CONTENTS

D0544655

CONTENTS

PART THREE

CRITICAL APPROACHES

PART FOUR

EXTENDED COMMENTARIES

PART ONE

INTRODUCTION

HOW TO STUDY A POEM

Studying on your own requires self-discipline and a carefully thought-out work plan in order to be effective.

- Poetry is the most challenging kind of literary writing. In your first reading you may well not understand what the poem is about. Don't jump too swiftly to any conclusions about the poem's meaning.
- Read the poem many times, and including out loud. After the second or third reading, write down any features you find interesting or unusual.
- What is the poem's tone of voice? What is the poem's mood?
- Does the poem have an argument? Is it descriptive?
- Is the poet writing in his or her own voice? Might he or she be using a persona or mask?
- Is there anything special about the kind of language the poet has chosen? Which words stand out? Why?
- What elements are repeated? Consider alliteration, assonance, rhyme, rhythm, metaphor and ideas.
- What might the poem's images suggest or symbolise?
- What might be significant about the way the poem is arranged in lines? Is there a regular pattern of lines? Does the grammar coincide with the ending of the lines or does it 'run over'? What is the effect of this?
- Do not consider the poem in isolation. Can you compare and contrast the poem with any other work by the same poet or with any other poem that deals with the same theme?
- What do you think the poem is about?
- Every argument you make about the poem must be backed up with details and quotations that explore its language and organisation.
- Always express your ideas in your own words.

This York Note offers an introduction to the poetry of *John Donne* and cannot substitute for close reading of the text and the study of secondary sources.

Here are the opening lines of five poems by Donne. The first three are all love poems, from a group known as the *Songs and Sonets*, while the fourth and fifth are from his *Divine Poems*:

> I wonder by my troth, what thou, and I
> Did, till we lov'd? ... ('The Good-morrow')

> Deare Love, for nothing lesse than thee
> Would I have broke this happy dreame ... ('The Dreame')

> When by thy scorne, O murdresse, I am dead ... ('The Apparition')

> Death be not proud, though some have called thee
> Mighty and dreadfull, for, thou art not soe ... (Holy Sonnet 'Death be not proud')

> This is my playes last scene, here heavens appoint
> My pilgrimage's last mile ... (Holy Sonnet 'This is my playes last scene')

The point here is not simply that John Donne had the knack of writing good first lines (though he did), but that this is a voice which still catches our attention, despite the gap of four centuries. The gap does exist, of course. Donne's language is often difficult, and the ideas he uses or explores in the poems are often complex as well as unfamiliar. For both of these reasons, Donne's poetry has sometimes been approached through a discussion of literary history, and with the aid of what might seem rather forbiddingly technical terms – among others, **wit**, **conceit**, **metaphysical**, the dissociation of sensibility. One of the aims of this Note is to offer help with these kinds of difficulty, but the reader coming to Donne for the first time would do well to set these terms aside for the moment, and to look instead for what seems to speak most immediately to us.

Consider an example. In the first of the poems quoted above, 'The Good-morrow', Donne begins to wrestle with a question which other lovers have faced, if not always faced up to. He is sure that this love is different from any he has previously known, but lovers often feel that, and the fact remains that they have each loved before. What does that mean for the relationship they are about to begin now? If they have loved, and left, others in the past, what security can they have for the future?

The second of the two *Divine Poems* quoted above provides another example. In this poem Donne forces himself to imagine not the beginning of a new love but the end of his life, the moment when body and soul are separated, the one to rot in the earth, the other to await God's judgement. Is this a time of fear, or of hope? Where is the borderline between the proper fear which leads the Christian believer to turn away from sin, and the improper fear which becomes despair, and leads on to doubt in God's love?

Although one of these is a secular poem, and the other a religious one, they clearly have something in common, which we feel in the voice, or, if you prefer, which we sense as a quality of the man who stands behind the poems. What we feel, I think, is that he brings to bear in each poem the full force of his passion and his intelligence. Few if any of Donne's poems can be seen as a simple cry from the heart; they neither are, nor pretend to be, raw expressions of emotion. Equally, very few look like pieces of argument which might have been put in prose, but instead have been turned into verse. In order to read them, we have to call on our own passion and intelligence. In the last analysis, Donne's poems are difficult because they are about the relationships of men and women with each other, and about the human relationship with God: and these are difficult issues.

There is then no short and easy way to become master of John Donne's poetry, but the poems are not so hard to understand and enjoy as is sometimes supposed. There are two pieces of essential advice: first, always to consider each poem separately; and second, always to begin by reading the poem in question aloud.

To take the first point, first: always consider each poem separately. Do not be too eager to establish generalisations about Donne's work as a whole, or to divide the poems into groups according to mood or theme, or to seize on one poem as so central or so characteristic that it can be made to provide a 'key' to all the others. While such approaches may seem to promise clarity, they lead almost inevitably to distortions – for example, to think of the poems as falling into groups is often to overlook the fact that Donne tackles the same theme with different degrees of success in different poems.

In learning how to confront each of Donne's poems individually, it is helpful to hold in mind a phrase used by F.R. Leavis (in *Revaluation*, Chatto and Windus, London, 1936), celebrating what he called Donne's 'irresistible rightness of tone', and then go on to ask a series of related questions about each poem. Firstly, about its 'rightness': what is it that Donne is trying to be right about, and how successful is he? Secondly, about the 'tone': what lies behind, and what is the effect of, the tone – or, more often, the changes of tone – in a given poem? In one way or another, these questions are raised in the accounts of individual poems in Part Four of this Note (Extended Commentaries). As part of your reading of Donne you might want to make use of the same questions in order to give an account of (say) 'Loves Growth' or 'A Valediction: forbidding mourning', or of 'Batter my heart' or 'A Hymne to Christ' from among the religious poems.

The second piece of advice is simply stated: always begin by reading the poems aloud. The seeming irregularity of Donne's **rhythmic** effects has been a source of difficulty to many readers. The basic pulse of his verse is clearly **iambic**, that is, it has a pattern of alternating unstressed and stressed syllables. We can find a simple example in 'The Will': 'To him for whom the passing bell next tolls, / I leave my physick bookes …'. Here the second of each pair of syllables clearly requires a stronger stress or emphasis. It would in fact be an extremely complex task to devise a system of formal rules which would explain how we should read each and every line of his verse, but there is no need to do so. At the cost of some simplification, the problem can be put like this: the iambic line is felt to be regular when the difference in weight or emphasis between the alternate unstressed and stressed syllables is strongly marked, as it was in most Elizabeth verse, and as it was to be again from (roughly) the later seventeenth century until the close of the nineteenth. But while Donne is occasionally regular in this way, as in the lines just quoted from 'The Will', he often gives more weight to the relatively unstressed syllables than most of his contemporaries would have expected, or, in some cases, tolerated. The reader of most Elizabethan verse grows accustomed to moving in a series of gentle steps, as if across a level lawn:

> One day I wrote her name upon the strand,
> But came the waves and washéd it away:
> Agayne I wrote it with a second hand,
> But came the tyde, and made my paynes his pray
> (Edmund Spenser, *Amoretti*, Sonnet LXXV, 1595)

But in many of John Donne's poems the words are packed together like boulders along a rocky coastline, and the reader has to learn how to clamber from one to another, as in 'A Nocturnall upon S. Lucies Day':

> All others, from all things, draw all that's good,
>
> Life, soule, forme, spirit, whence they beeing have;
>
> I, by loves limbecke am the grave
>
> Of all, that's nothing. Oft a flood
>
> Have wee two wept, and so
>
> Drownd the whole world, us two; oft did we grow
>
> To be two Chaosses, when we did show
>
> Care to ought else; and often absences
>
> Withdrew our soules, and made us carcasses.

A note made in 1811 by the poet and critic Samuel Taylor Coleridge (1772–1834) provides all the help that is necessary. Coleridge wrote that when reading Donne's poems 'full use should be made of pause, hurrying of voice, or apt and sometimes double emphasis', and the aim should always be to 'bring out the sense of passion more prominently'. In other words, an understanding of the drama of the verse will almost always guide the reader to an understanding of its rhythmic character; and, correspondingly, to discover how to read the verse aloud will almost always afford clues to an understanding of its logic and structure.

READING THE *SONGS AND SONETS*

For many modern readers the *Songs and Sonets* are among the three or four finest collections of love poems in the English language. Yet in all periods there have been distinguished readers unable to accept this high estimate. In the seventeenth century the poet John Dryden (1631–1700) declared that 'Donne perplexes the minds of the fair sex with nice speculations of philosophy, when he should engage their hearts and entertain them with the softness of love'. Samuel Johnson (1709–84), one of the greatest of English critics, voiced similar doubts. In his 'Life of Cowley' (1779) Johnson, borrowing the term from Dryden, described as 'the **metaphysical** poets' a group of seventeenth-century poets who, whether or not directly influenced by Donne, shared something of his poetic manner and **idiom**. Johnson alleged that these poets, including Donne, wrote of human life as if they had no share or involvement in it: 'The metaphysical poets were men of learning, and to show their learning was their whole endeavour ... Their courtship was void of fondness, and their lamentation of sorrow ... they never attempted that comprehension and expanse of thought which at once fills the whole mind, and of which the first effect is sudden astonishment, and the second rational admiration.' In the twentieth century this complaint has been taken further by the scholar C.S. Lewis, who argued that 'Donne's love poetry ... largely omits the very thing that all the pother was about': in other words, the *Songs and Sonets* are a kind of love poetry in which the love is missed out.

These are substantial charges. In effect, the critics quoted here are agreed on three points: firstly, that the difficulties of 'metaphysical poetry', including Donne's, are merely superficial ('to show their learning was their whole endeavour'); secondly, that such poetry is unable adequately to portray human feelings ('their courtship was void of fondness'); and thirdly, that such poetry cannot succeed in engaging the interest of the reader at the deepest levels ('that comprehension and expanse of thought which at once fills the whole mind'). To quote C.S. Lewis once more: 'Paradoxical as it may seem, Donne's poetry is too simple to satisfy ... there is none of the depth and ambiguity of real experience in him.' Clearly those who believe John Donne to be a major poet have to make a stand at this point; they have to demonstrate that Donne is, in fact, more truthfully alive to the complexity of 'real experience' than his detractors have supposed. This can only be done convincingly by means of analyses of individual poems, and to that end five of the *Songs and Sonets* are examined in detail in Extended Commentaries: 'The Sunne rising', 'The Apparition', 'The Good-morrow', 'Loves Alchymie', and 'The Anniversarie'. As a preliminary, it is useful to look first at one feature for which most readers would allow that the *Songs and Sonets* are remarkable: that is, the variety of feelings expressed in the collection as a whole.

This variety is easily established. The first poem in the first printed edition (1633) was 'The Good-morrow', which develops out of a sense of discovery: the two lovers, their various false starts now behind them, have found together what real love is, and the poet suggests that here at last is a love that will survive even in a world dominated by change. Next comes the 'Song' written to fit an existing melody, 'Goe, and catche a falling starre': a cynical but cheerful claim that 'No where / Lives a woman true, and faire'. Third is 'Womans Constancy', in which the poet cites various false arguments his mistress might use to cast him off, and claims that the only reason he does not at once prove them false is that he might want to use them himself in order to reject her. The first three poems thus deal in turn with constant love, female fickleness, and the corresponding fickleness of men.

The next two poems take contrasting views of the importance of sexual expression in love. 'The Undertaking' is a poem of Platonic love in which the poet argues that he is among those few who can recognise and love the 'lovelinesse within', and therefore have no interest in the lesser joys of physical love; the next poem, 'The Sunne rising', celebrates the pleasures of a satisfied love in extravagant terms: the woman is 'all States', and he, her lover, is accordingly 'all Princes', while the sun which wakes them is paltry in comparison with them. In the two following poems, 'The Indifferent' and 'Loves Usury', the poet either dismisses or attacks the idea of fidelity; in the next, 'The Canonization', he is found arguing that the poet and his lady are ideally constant lovers who deserve to be worshipped as saints in the religion of love.

And so it goes on throughout the collection, no one poem ever quite repeating the mood of the other. The sense of this variety of feeling is somewhat reduced if we follow those critics who wish to divide the *Songs and Sonets* into two groups: roughly, a group collecting the more or less cynical and promiscuous poems, which are presumed to be earlier, and a group of more obviously thoughtful or idealistic poems, presumed to have been written after Donne's marriage in 1601. But even then the sense of variety is inescapable, if only because Donne's poetry draws on so many fields of reference: the bite of a flea and the music of the spheres, geography and astronomy, medieval theology and medicine, military manoeuvres, alchemy, taxation, the riddle of the Phoenix and the King's delight in hunting, all make their way into the *Songs and Sonets*. Love, for Donne, does not exist isolated from other emotions and activities (as it does in the work of some poets), but alongside and mingled with them.

Consequently, in his poetry love appears under many aspects, from the assurance of 'The Sunne rising' to the anger of 'The Apparition' and the desolation of 'A Nocturnall upon S. Lucies Day'. To read the *Songs and Sonets* through is to receive the irresistible impression that love is not one simple thing but a compound of many: 'mixt of all stuffes, paining soule, or sense', and not 'pure, and abstract' ('Loves Growth'). It is partly the range and strength of feeling exhibited in these poems that reveals Donne as a love-lyricist of the very highest order, and most modern readers would regard the *Songs and Sonets* not only as his major achievement, but also as one of the major achievements of English poetry.

READING *THE DIVINE POEMS*

Part of the temptation to group John Donne's poems comes from the fact that he is one of the great religious poets, as well as one of the great poets of sexual love. There are clear similarities between the secular and the religious poems – they have in common the instinct towards argument, the sense of personal confrontation with another (Donne addresses his God as directly as he addresses the women in his poems), the feeling we have that the whole man is present in the verse – but most of the *Divine Poems* come from the middle and later period of his life, and the strain of those years of disappointment, ill-health and financial insecurity is often evident. While there are many poems celebrating the joys of sexual life, or written out of the experience of certain and fulfilled love, it is hard to find religious poems to compare with these – for example, poems celebrating moments of vision in which the poet glimpses his ultimate union with God or feels a renewed assurance of the promise of heavenly bliss. Rather, the *Divine Poems* are typically marked by an effort of the will, in which Donne seeks to examine and discipline his mind, and in many of them the freedom and vitality so characteristic of the love poetry are replaced by a mood which borders on despair.

It has seemed to some readers that even the best known of the *Divine Poems* have about them something forced and overdramatic. The explanation for this may lie in the tradition of meditation, which underlies a number of the poems. The meditation is a form of religious exercise in which memory and imagination are used systematically to help focus and encourage a mood of devotion: for example, a meditation on the theme of God's love might begin with an attempt to imagine the sufferings of Christ on the Cross, while a meditation on the theme of God's eventual judgement on mankind might begin with an attempt to imagine the fears one might feel during the night before one's death. When Donne begins a poem with the question, 'What if this present were the worlds last night?', the intention is to force himself – and thus the reader – to face what he regarded as an inevitable reality: the moment when the world comes to an end, and every man and woman has to stand before God, and learn whether he or she is saved or damned. The more vividly Donne can summon the **image** of this event before our minds, the less likely it is that our response to it will be perfunctory or self-deceiving.

The reader of Donne's poetry quickly discovers that Donne is unable to leave any idea or any experience unexamined. If he falls in love, he wants to understand what 'love' means; if he uses the word 'now', he is drawn to think about the past and the future too. The same questioning, and questing, habit of mind is found in the religious poems. If, after his death, Donne is re-born, as the Christian tradition suggests, in what ways will the new Donne be the same as the one who lived out his life on earth? Is the body resurrected, or only the soul? If each man and woman is judged by God at the moment of death, what happens between that moment and the general Day of Judgement when the world is brought to an end? These questions are not, for Donne, merely intellectual puzzles; these are issues for which men and women in his time were ready to go to the stake.

The best of John Donne's poetry, then – and among the *Divine Poems*, this includes the sonnet 'Since she whome I lov'd', 'A Hymne to Christ', and 'A Hymne to God the Father' – is marked by a passionate intensity, which can excite, move and trouble the reader. His love poems stand comparison with Shakespeare's *Sonnets*, or with Thomas Hardy's elegies for the death of his first wife; along with the Victorian poet Gerard Manley Hopkins, he is the great English poet of the crisis between faith and doubt. It is a mark of the greatest poems that we feel driven to give an account of them, at the same time that we know any such account will be inadequate beside the poem itself. Underlying this Note is the conviction that Donne writes great poems of this kind.

PART TWO

COMMENTARIES

The first edition of John Donne's poems was published two years after his death, in 1633. This was not an edition planned or supervised by Donne, and there is no reason to suppose that the order in which the poems appeared was one Donne had chosen himself. However, Donne's twentieth-century editors have generally agreed that the 1633 edition is authoritative about the texts of the poems. Previously they had been circulated in manuscript form, passed around from friend to friend, copied and recopied – and, inevitably, sometimes miscopied. In some cases large groups of poems appear together, in others there are only a few. Donne's sonnet on the death of his wife, 'Since she whome I lovd', is not in the 1633 edition, and is found only in one manuscript; it was first published in 1894, with a misreading – a useful reminder to those who doubt that copyists make errors. However, in other cases study of the surviving manuscripts suggests that some variant readings may indicate not an error by the copyist, but a change of mind by Donne himself. There is, then, room for doubt in at least a few cases about the ideal text.

The text used for this Note is *John Donne: Selected Poems* edited with an introduction by John Hayward, The Penguin Poetry Library, 1950. This applies also to the spellings, which are those used in the 1633 edition – including the title *Songs and Sonets*, with a single 'n' – which has the advantage of revealing where the older spelling suggested a link between words which modern spellings might obscure. Within the limits of this Note, however, it was not possible to annotate all the poems included by Hayward, and a further selection had to be made. This further selection reflects the choice of poems in Helen Gardner's influential anthology *The Metaphysical Poets*, in the revised edition published by Penguin in 1972. In one or two cases, the annotation has taken account of Gardner's readings. Two of the poems included by Gardner, the Holy Sonnets 'As due by many titles' and 'Oh my black soule', are not given by Hayward, but are annotated and briefly discussed here because recent scholarship suggests that they form part of a sequence of meditations on sin and judgement. The other poems appear in both Gardner and Hayward, and it is hoped that this Note will be of use to a reader using either of these, or indeed other, editions.

SATYRE: ON RELIGION

John Donne wrote five *Satyres* during the early 1590s: this, the third, probably dates from around 1594–5. A **satire** is generally defined as a piece of writing in which vices or follies are held up to ridicule, but only the first part of the present poem is satirical in this sense. The argument falls into three sections: a condemnation of those who fail to seek for religious truth (lines 1–42); encouragement to seek 'true religion' despite the doubts and conflicts of an age of religious controversy (lines 43–87); and a warning that it is better to risk persecution for disobeying the secular authorities, than to risk damnation by betraying the truth reached by the efforts of the individual conscience. At the time he was writing this poem Donne was, according to his first biographer, 'unresolved what religion to adhere to', and the twists and turns in the argument suggest how difficult it was to choose between the Catholic and Protestant positions (see Historical Background).

It is sometimes suggested that Donne learned his poetic skills from the example of the London theatres, but in this poem the **verse** is handled with a freedom and assurance that was not to be heard on the stage until the end of the 1590s; see especially lines 79–88, where the **rhythm** suggests both the difficulty of the struggle to discover the truth, and the urgency of the need to do so.

> **Kinde pitty ... / Those teares to issue** the 'sins' he is about to consider demand his pity for those who are his fellow human beings, but they also provoke his contempt, so that the two impulses check each other
>
> **be wise** the wise course is neither to laugh at sins nor to weep over them
>
> **railing** abusing
>
> **worne maladies** faults which have been present for a long time
>
> **the first blinded age** the age of pagan philosophy, before the light of the Christian revelation

Are not heavens joyes ... / earths honour was to them? can the promise of bliss in heaven not calm our desires, as the hope of honour on earth calmed those of the pagan philosophers?

As wee do them in meanes ... / Us in the end we have the advantage over the pagans in possessing the means of getting to heaven (the Christian revelation); may they nonetheless surpass us in achieving the end, and getting there, while we fail and go – elsewhere?

whose merit / ... may be imputed faith the merit of their virtuous lives may be allowed to make up for the faith they necessarily lacked, but which was otherwise necessary for salvation. See the note on 'imputed grace' in the commentary accompanying 'Elegie: To his Mistris Going to Bed'

so easie wayes and neare such easy and direct ways

ayd mutinous Dutch at the end of the sixteenth century a number of English soldiers went to assist ('aid') the Dutch in their war against the Spanish

leaders rage the unpredictable temper of a military commander

dearth famine, shortage of supplies

frozen North discoveries the known existence of a south-west passage into the Pacific led sixteenth-century explorers to seek a corresponding north-west route

Salamanders lizard-like animals supposed to be able to live in fire

like divine / Children in th'oven in the Old Testament story Shadrach, Meshach and Abednego walked unharmed in the fiery furnace into which they were thrown by Nebuchadnezzar, the king of Babylon (see Daniel 3)

fires of Spaine the Spanish Inquisition handed over heretics to be burned; those who fought against them for the Dutch would be considered heretics

and the line the heat of the equator (the 'line')

limbecks alembics, used in distilling (a process which requires the use of great heat)

must every hee / ... words? must every person who will not hail your mistress as a goddess draw his sword to fight, or else endure your insults and abuse?

and his and God's

Sentinell soldier on guard duty

forbidden warres wars whose purposes are merely worldly

appointed field the moral battleground, where every Christian was required to fight on God's side against the forces of evil

The foule Devill ... / to be quit the devil would gladly surrender his whole kingdom of Hell to you, but out of hate rather than love, in order to rid himself of it

The worlds all parts all the parts of the world

the worlds selfe the world itself

In her decrepit wayne the world was believed to be in its wane, that is, running down

last finally

Flesh (it selfes death) the flesh is the cause of its own death, because the sins of the flesh lead to death

Mirreus myrrh gives incense its smell. Mirreus is therefore the man who loves incense, which was used in the Roman Catholic Church

unhous'd here rejected here, in Protestant Britain

her ragges the few scraps of the original truth still recognised by the Roman Church

wee here obey / The statecloth in England it was the custom to bow to the throne even when the monarch was not present

Crantz presumably chosen as a representative German sounding name, the Reformation movement having begun in Germany

brave ostentatious, showy (the Roman Church used a more elaborate form of ritual than the Reformed churches)

inthrall'd enslaved, won over

Geneva Geneva was the home of the Puritan John Calvin (1509–64), and was organised along rigorously Protestant lines

yong the Protestant churches belonged to the sixteenth century whereas the Church of Rome claimed to go back to Christ's disciple, St Peter

Lecherous humors tastes in lechery

wholsome attractive

drudges working girls

Graius a Greek. It is not clear why John Donne chooses the name

ambitious bauds ambitious pimps, paid for procuring lovers for their mistress, and therefore willing to say anything in her praise, however false or exaggerated

lawes / Still new like fashions a number of laws were passed to regulate religious practice during the reign of Elizabeth I

is onely perfect is the only perfect one

Imbraceth embraces, chooses

Godfathers spiritual guides

Tender to him offer to him

being tender while or because he is weak and young

as Wards still / ... Pay valewes as wards accept the marriage arranged for them by their guardians, or else pay a fine. Elizabeth's Act of Uniformity (1559) imposed fines on recusants, that is, on those who refused to attend the parish church

Carelesse unconcerned

Phrygius a Phrygian, from the ancient country of Asia Minor. It is not clear why John Donne chooses the name

Graccus member of the Roman family of that name. John Donne perhaps uses it because in the second century BC several members of the family were distinguished for their personal integrity and desire to act justly

All ... as one equally

divers habits different costumes

one kinde of one species

So doth, so is Religion religion may appear in different forms in different countries, but is in fact everywhere one and the same

this blind- / nesse too much light breeds believing that every religion has the light of truth, he is blinded to the point where he cannot distinguish true from false

unmoved not easily led astray by momentary feelings

Of force must one, and forc'd but one allow you must necessarily admit one religion as the true one, and even under pressure must not admit any other as true

aske thy father ... / a little elder is John Donne is referring to the words of Moses to the people of Israel: 'Ask thy father, and he will shew thee; thy elders, and they will tell thee' (see the Bible, Deuteronomy 32:7). The suggestion is, that it is necessary to recover the original truth, which was once revealed but has now been obscured or forgotten

Hee's not of none, nor worst, that seekes the best the man who pauses to seek the true religion is not a man of no religion, nor of the worst religion

To adore, or scorne an image, or protest to be a Roman Catholic, an anti-Catholic, or a Protestant

in strange way / To stand inquiring right to pause when one is lost to consider which is the right road

To sleepe, or runne wrong, is to give up the search, or to choose too hastily, is certainly the way to go wrong in the end

Cragged steep, rugged

about must, and about must goe must travel by a gradual and roundabout path in order to make his way

suddennes steepness

rest make its final choice

none can worke in that night from the warning given in the New Testament that 'the night cometh, when no man can work' (see John 9:4)

To will to be going to, to consider this as a task for the future

Hard deeds ... / indeavours reach hard deeds are done through hard physical work, and hard knowledge is gained through strenuous mental effort

mysteries / ... to all eyes we cannot help seeing the sun, even though we cannot look at it directly; in the same way we know that there are religious truths, or 'mysteries', even though the mind cannot comprehend them fully

men do not stand / ... hangmen to Fate our situation is not so desperate that God has given the authorities a free hand to persecute just as they wish; they are merely the instruments of Fate, carrying out the will of God and not their own

let thy Soule be tyed / To mans lawes allow your choice of religion to be made for you by man-made laws

boot thee do you any good

Philip ... Gregory / A Harry, or a Martin Philip II of Spain, a deeply Catholic monarch; Gregory XIV, the then Pope; Henry VIII, the founder of the English Church; Martin Luther (1483–1548), who published in 1517 his Ninety-five Theses upon Indulgences, sometimes said to have begun the Reformation

Is not this excuse ... / Equally strong? will this excuse not serve equally well for opposite religious groups?

That thou mayest ... / is idolatrie it was widely agreed that secular authorities were entitled to require a certain measure of obedience, but also that there was a limit to what could be demanded; to exceed that limit was to change a proper authority into tyranny. How to fix that limit was an endlessly debated question, and John Donne is not really providing an answer

As streames are, Power is ... / in the sea are lost the argument is, that all power comes from God (the 'calme head' or source). Some authorities rule in accordance with God's laws, and those who obey them will prosper: some other authorities (likened here to a stream at a distance from the calm source) ignore God's will, and those who allow themselves to be driven by these godless authorities will be destroyed

In Helen Gardner's major edition of John Donne's love poetry fourteen poems are printed as *Elegies*. In modern usage the term **elegy** is generally reserved for poems of lamentation for the dead, but in the sixteenth and seventeenth centuries it could be applied to almost any reflective poem written in a regular **metre** (in Donne's case, **rhyming couplets**). Donne's *Elegies* belong to the mid-1590s, and probably owe their inspiration to the *Amores*, or love poems, of the Roman poet Ovid (43BC–AD18). One main tradition of sixteenth-century love poetry was the **Petrarchan** one, so named after the early Italian poet Francesco Petrarca (1304–74), whose poems often provided the model for English imitations. In this tradition the woman addressed is idealised, and the lover is cast in the role of a suffering (and often complaining) servant. The Ovidian tradition, however, was realistic, dramatic and direct, and no doubt appealed to Donne precisely because of its non-Petrarchan character. Five of the *Elegies*, including 'On his Mistris' and 'To his Mistris going to Bed', were evidently considered too direct, and the licenser, or censor, refused permission for them to be printed in the first edition of Donne's poems in 1633.

H IS PICTURE

The poet presents his mistress with a miniature portrait of himself, before leaving on a voyage; if he should either die abroad, or return disfigured by the hardships of the journey, it will remind her, and prove to others, what he once was. Donne took part in military expeditions in 1596 and 1597, though there is no need to associate the poem with an event in his life.

The implied comparison at the end of the poem, between milk and young love, meat and adult love, is a characteristic example of the kind of complex reasoning which delighted Donne, but seemed to some later readers inappropriate where the subject was love.

> **take my Picture** presumably a miniature portrait of himself
> **but I dead** when I am dead
> **shadowes both** the word 'shadows' could be applied to ghosts, and to images or portraits
> **rude** clumsily constructed
> **hairecloth** coarse cloth made of hair

With cares ... o'rspread when stress and hardships have turned his hair prematurely grey

powders blew staines blue gunpowder stains

taxe thee criticise you, demand an explanation from you

foule ugly

reach affect. She will not be harmed by changes in his appearance

That which in him ... / ...seemes tough the comparison is between milk for babies and meat for adults. He suggests that if she is challenged to defend her choice of him, she will explain that while her young love was indeed fed by his outward beauty, her more mature love is able to be nourished by her sense of the whole man. Those with less experience of love would be unable to manage this mature response

ON HIS MISTRIS

The poet, about to leave on a journey to continental Europe, urges his mistress to set aside their vows to stay together despite all dangers, and to wait for him in England rather than (as she seems to have suggested) dressing herself as a (boy) page in order to follow him. What Donne speaks of here as his 'words masculine perswasive force' is evident in all the *Elegies*; if it's sometimes overwhelming, it is also, at least implicitly, a compliment to the woman, who is always assumed to be the man's intellectual equal.

strange when they were strangers to one another

fatall significant, momentous

remorse pity, compassion

Begot created

want and divorcement want of each other, and separation

I conjure thee I solemnly beg you

to seal joynt constanccy to guarantee our fidelity to each other

Temper calm down

impetuous rage excited and over-hasty passion

faign'd pretended

onely worthy ... / Thirst to come back only you could create and develop in me a longing to return

else otherwise

Boreas in Greek mythology, the god of the North wind

Thou hast reade / ... he lov'd the myths in fact tell how Boreas carried Orithea away when her father refused them permission to marry, but not that she came to any harm as a consequence

Fall ill ... / Dangers unurg'd whether the outcome is fortunate or not, it is madness to endure dangers not forced upon them

Feede on this flattery believe this fiction, that is, console yourself by believing what you know is untrue

Dissemble nothing do not pretend anything, or disguise yourself in any way

not a boy do not pretend to be a boy

nor change / ... nor mindes do not change your clothes, or alter your mind

bee not strange / To thy selfe onely if she disguised herself as a boy, she would feel strange to herself, but everyone else would immediately see through the disguise

as soone / Ecclips'd as bright the moon is still the moon, whether shining brightly or in eclipse

Camelions chameleons, reptiles which are able to change the colour of their skin to suit their surroundings

Spittles hospitals, especially those for the treatment of venereal diseases. Syphilis was known as the 'French disease'

Loves fuellers those who deliberately encourage passion in themselves

Players actors were generally associated with an immoral way of life

knowe thee, and no lesse both see through your disguise, and sexually possess you (the verb 'to know' was commonly used for sexual coition); in some manuscripts this line reads 'knowe thee, 'and knowe thee'

Th'indifferent Italian the Italian is here assumed to be equally willing to ravish either a boy or a girl, so her disguise will still not protect her. It was presumably this passage which made the licenser uneasy

As *Lots* faire guests were vext in the Old Testament story Lot entertained two angels in his house in Sodom, but the Sodomites supposed them to be two beautiful young men, and demanded to be allowed to ravish them (see Genesis 19)

spongy hydroptique drunken (hydropsy, or dropsy, is a disease associated with an insatiable thirst)

displease harm, distress

England is onely a worthy Gallerie England is the only proper gallery for her (the ante-room for those waiting to see the sovereign was called a gallery)

Our greatest King God

blesse nor curse / Openly loves force do not speak in public of the power of love, either to praise it or to complain of it

midnights startings nightmares

Assail'd attacked

Augure me better chance he does not wish her fears for his safety to be an ill omen, predicting harm to him

except lest, in case

enough that is, enough happiness, or good 'chance'

To his mistris going to bed

The most satisfactory parts of this poem are probably those which most freely express the poet's sexual desire, as he watches his mistress undress for bed. The legal and theological **imagery** seems to be present less because it is appropriate to this particular poem (and if, as the opening lines perhaps suggest, the lady is a prostitute, the imagery is definitely inappropriate), than because Donne wished in a general way to mock the more solemn **Petrarchan** poems of his time.

How we respond to this poem (and to many of Donne's love poems) depends to some degree on whether we imagine it as addressed to a real woman, or as written for the amusement of an audience of male friends. But however we take it, we might note that Donne assumes here, as elsewhere, that the language of sexual love is not a special lovers' language; rather, it includes any idea that comes to hand, whether drawn from the ordinary realities of daily life, or from the wide range of his reading. The dramatic situation of the poems presents the woman primarily as a sexual partner for the man, and some readers may feel uneasy about this; but the language and range of reference typically also assume that she is intelligent, witty and confident, and that she is sexually as enthusiastic and experienced as he is.

all rest my powers defie his powers, or sexual energies, prevent him from settling down to rest

I in labour lie he waits impatiently, as a woman in labour awaits the delivery of her baby

The foe … the foe the male and female sexual organs, imagined as waiting to join battle

standing keeping erect and ready

heavens Zone the outermost sphere of the universe carried the fixed stars, which would appear like a belt across the heavens

spangled breastplate the stomacher, or front-piece of a dress, covering the breast and the pit of the stomach, and often decorated with jewels

busie prying, intruding

harmonious chyme she is wearing a chiming watch

that happy busk … stand so nigh he envies her corset, which, stiffened with whalebone, can remain stiff indefinitely, even though so close to her. He begins to fear that he might not he able to match it. See the note above on 'standing'

steales goes quietly away

Coronet a metal band worn around the forehead

Diademe diadem, or head-band, often decorated with jewels

Mahomets Paradice heaven made up of entirely sensual pleasures (John Donne is following contemporary ideas about Islamic teaching)

and though / Ill spirits walk in white even if evil spirits disguise themselves by wearing white garments

these Angels women

Those set our hairs, but these the flesh upright this is a third joke about the male erection. Evil spirits make only the hair stand on end (through fear)

safeliest when with one man man'd most safe when inhabited or possessed by one man only

Emperie the territory owned by an emperor

bonds commitments, or more simply, her arms. John Donne probably has in mind the familiar Christian idea, that perfect freedom is only to be found in the service of Christ

where my hand is set, my seal shall be he has put his hand on her as if signing a contract between them (compare 'bonds', in the previous line), and he will now consummate their love, as if confirming a contract with the imprint of his seal

As souls unbodied … / whole joyes as souls must free themselves of their bodies in order to taste the joys of heaven, so lovers' bodies must be free of their clothes to gain the fullest bliss

Atlanta's balls, cast in mens views in the story by Ovid, Atlanta would only marry a man who could beat her in a foot-race. Hippomenes distracted her by throwing three golden balls down in front of her, and so won the race. John Donne rather muddles his comparison by having men fall victim to the strategies of women

theirs what merely belongs to them

lay-men the uneducated majority, who are content to admire the outward show, such as a woman's jewelry or the bright covers of a book, and so fail to appreciate the greater value of the woman herself, or the book's contents

mystick mystic, containing secrets which only the dedicated few will be able to discover

imputed grace John Donne is here borrowing an idea from the theology of Calvin. Calvin argued that men were unable to win salvation through any merit of their own, but a few were chosen by God to be saved because the righteousness or 'grace' of Jesus Christ was 'imputed' or credited to them – that is, they were saved for merits which were not strictly their own. John Donne is suggesting that no man deserves the joy he longs for with a woman, but can only hope that the woman will impute to him her own infinitely superior qualities, and love him for them

liberally freely, unreservedly

Here is no pennance, much less innocence the colour white was associated with penitence and with virginity; the lady of this poem, therefore, has no reason to keep on her white nightgown

more covering than a man there are two meanings here: (a) more covering than the poet himself is wearing; (b) anything else to cover her than a man

FROM *THE SONGS AND SONETS*

The second edition of John Donne's poems (1635) collected together a group of love **lyrics** as *Songs and Sonets*, although only six of the poems are 'songs' in the sense that they were written to fit existing tunes, and none of them are formally **sonnets** (that is, poems fourteen lines in length). They range in length from ten to seventy-two lines, and include simple **quatrains** as well as highly elaborate **stanza** forms, some of them unique to Donne. All but one are assumed to be spoken by a male speaker (the exception is 'Breake of Day', where the speaker is a woman), and typically there is a strong sense of the presence of the person supposed to be addressed, whether directly as 'The Good-morrow', or by implication, as in 'Twicknam Garden'. There is no reason to suppose that the order in which the poems appear was chosen by Donne, nor that they should be read as a sequence: indeed, while a number of ideas appear in different poems, most readers are more struck by the sense of diversity than of unity.

In Helen Gardner's major edition of the love poetry, fifty-four poems appear as *Songs and Sonets*. None of them can be dated with certainty, although Gardner argues for a distinction between an earlier group (written before 1600), and a later group (written after 1602). Other readers of Donne have also wished to classify the love poems in some way; Theodore Redpath, for example, in the Introduction to his very helpful edition of *The Songs and Sonets of John Donne* (1956), divides the poems into two main groups, according to whether the predominating attitude in them is 'negative' or 'positive', with various sub-classes within the two main categories.

Such arguments are understandable, but there are possible dangers here for the unwary reader. The most obvious of these is the assumption that each individual poem directly reflects some episode in the poet's life which was, in effect, the cause of the poem. We have no warrant for interpreting Donne's life in terms of the poetry, or the poetry by means of what we believe we know of the life. Donne's was a complex character; his moods and interests were clearly as varied as the poems themselves, and we should not allow a desire to classify the poems to reduce and simplify our image of the man who wrote them.

For the same reason, we should be cautious in trying to define Donne's attitude to love. The assumption in 'The Flea', for example, is that the only thing which matters is sexual satisfaction; the poem is a battle of wits, and the prize is the woman's presumed surrender to the poet's demands. In contrast to this is 'A Valediction: forbidding mourning', where the poet scorns 'Dull sublunary lovers love', and celebrates a love so 'refin'd' or spiritualised that mere physical absence cannot diminish its perfection. Both these attitudes are echoed in other poems. Similarly, in a number of poems Donne claims that love is immune to change, but in as many others the claim for the lovers' supremacy over the temporal world is accompanied by an acute sense of their vulnerability in a world dominated by time. It seems pointless to ask which of these are his 'real' views; all we can say with certainty is that he expressed different attitudes in different poems according to the mood of the moment. However, it may be said that so many of the *Songs and Sonets* assert the dignity of love, and its claim on the entire self – both body and soul – that it may be that it is in these poems that the reader comes closest to discovering John Donne's usual feelings about love.

The flea

The flea provided a popular subject for love poetry throughout Europe in the sixteenth century, following a medieval poem then attributed to the Roman poet Ovid. The poet usually envied the flea its freedom on his mistress's body, or its death at her hands while in the ecstasy of its contact with her. Donne discovers a variation on the motif, turning the fact that the flea bites both the man and the woman into a seduction game.

'The Flea' is characteristic of Donne's more flippant, sometimes cynical poems. On one level it is clearly unrealistic: men and women are not seduced by discussions about fleas. Yet on another, the sense of reality is precisely what we might want to draw attention to – for example, the way the poem catches the energy of the speaking voice (notice the use of questions and imperatives – 'Marke', 'Oh stay' – to move the poem onwards – in some manuscripts, there is a third, with 'Confess it' instead of 'Thou know'st' at the start of line 6), or the way it accepts that sexual relationships can include an element of play, even of competition.

There is a further point you might want to consider. The poem is presented as one half of a debate between a man and a woman. The real audience, however, and the real target for Donne's logical trickery, is the reader. Even so, the dramatic situation is that of a man winning an argument against a woman, who – we might think – only appears in the poem in order to lose. You will have to decide for yourself whether this is a limitation in the poem (though when thinking about this you might also want to look at 'The Sunne rising', in which the poet's silent opponent is the sun).

Marke observe

our two bloods mingled bee sexual intercourse was believed to involve the mingling of the blood of each of the partners

this enjoyes before it wooe the flea (unlike the woman) is satisfied without the trouble of a long courtship

pamper'd over-indulged

one blood made of two see the note on 'our two bloods' above

grudge complain, express reluctance

cloysterd a cloister is a covered walk in a religious building. The flea is seen here as a temple in which their marriage has taken place

Jet a deep glossy black

Though use make thee apt to kill mee though she is in the habit of killing him (by her refusal of him)

three sinnes in killing three (a) murder and (b) suicide because the blood of both is included in the flea, and (c) sacrilege because as a temple the flea is now a holy place

sodaine sudden, violent

Purpled stained with blood in killing the flea. In grand drama blood was often said to be purple

Yet thou triumph'st ... / ... tooke life from thee the lady argues that in killing the flea she has demonstrated the poet's arguments to be ridiculous, for no harm was done and no sins were committed. He turns her triumph against her by claiming that there will, similarly, be no harm done or sin committed when she eventually yields to him

THE GOOD-MORROW

This brief but complex poem is organised around two central **metaphors**, of a pair of lovers 'waking' into a new life together, and of the new 'world' created by their mutual love. Neither **image** was original to Donne: what makes the poem so characteristic is that the images are not used merely decoratively, to give poetic status to a simple idea, but argumentatively, to reveal more about the experience of love than was at first evident. For a fuller discussion, see Extended Commentaries where this poem is discussed in more detail.

by my troth truly

were we not wean'd till then? / ... childishly? the suggestion is that they have now passed together from the clumsy and immature sexual experiences of their past, into a more sophisticated and adult awareness. There is probably an indecent **pun** on 'countrey', as there is when Hamlet speaks of 'country matters' in Shakespeare's play (*Hamlet*, III.2.112)

snorted snored

seaven sleepers den the cave in which seven young Christians from Ephesus were walled up alive as they attempted to escape persecution by the emperor Decius. They awoke many years later to find that Christianity was now the officially accepted religion

But this, all pleasures fancies bee all other pleasures except this of their love are mere fancies, lacking reality

If ever any beauty ... / ... a dreame of thee the other beautiful women he had seen, desired, and possessed as mistresses, were only shadows or images of the reality he now finds completely expressed in her

good morrow good morning – the usual Elizabethan greeting. The lovers are waking up in bed together

For love ... controules true love removes the restless desire to see other people or places

one little roome, an every where this is an idea to which John Donne often returns, notably in 'The Sunne rising'

Let sea-discoverers ... / ... worlds on worlds have showne the two lovers refuse to be interested in the new worlds, or continents, discovered by explorers, or in the unexplored worlds revealed in the new maps of the heavens

Let us possesse ... and is one let us possess our world of mutual love; you are the world to me, as I am the world to you

My face ... appeares as implied in line 10, they are gazing at each other

plaine honest, undisguised

Where can we finde ... / ... declining West? her eye reflecting him, and his eye reflecting her, suggest the two hemispheres or half-worlds, which together make up one world. But here each hemisphere is special, or privileged: there is no cold Northern region, and no Western sunset leading on towards night. It would of course be impossible to construct a sphere consisting only of the South and the East; the logic is illusory, and John Donne expects us to recognise this

What ever dyes, was not mixt equally John Donne is alluding to the medieval and Elizabethan idea that decay and corruption result from the lack of perfect balance and proportion in the elements of which all bodies are constituted

If our two loves ... none can die variant readings in the manuscripts suggest that John Donne himself was not certain how to finish this poem. The sense is that whatever dies or decays does so because of some lack of balance or unity. If we really are one world, or if at any rate our two loves are so exactly matched that there can be no decay, then there can be no death of love

Song: goe, and catche a falling starre

Poems based on a list of impossible tasks were and are quite common, at both the sophisticated and the popular level. Here the ultimate impossibility is to find a woman who is both chaste and beautiful. On the face of it, this ought to be a disagreeably cynical poem, but the exaggeration of the last verse ('False, ere I come, to *two or three*' – emphasis added) suggests that it is to be read humourously, very much like some contemporary poems designed for public performance.

This is one of the poems said in some manuscripts to have been written to fit an existing tune.

a mandrake roote the mandrake has a forked root, and was believed to resemble the human form

who cleft the Divels foot the Devil was supposed to have a cleft, or divided, hoof

Mermaides mermaids (imaginary sea-creatures, having the face and body of a woman, but the tail of a fish) are often associated with song

to keep off envies stinging to protect myself from the attacks of jealous people

What winde / ... honest minde the suggestion is that honesty will never help one to advancement or promotion. The **rhymes** here (find, wind, mind) were correct until the eighteenth century

If thou beest borne to strange sights if you were born with the gift of second sight (which enables you to see 'things invisible' to others)

snow here used as a transitive verb: turn your hair white

befell thee happened to you

last remain true and chaste

THE UNDERTAKING, OR PLATONIC LOVE

The poet claims in this poem to have achieved an entirely pure and spiritual love, free from sensual desire. The Greek philosopher Plato (*c.*427–348BC) described such love, notably in his work *The Symposium:* hence the term 'Platonic Love'. That this poem can be seen as a direct contradiction of 'Goe, and catch a falling starre' suggests that Donne was interested in exploring different experiences of love; we do not know how far, if at all, either poem reflects his own personal life, nor do we need to know. However, Donne often uses the idea of love as a religious mystery, which he and his lady can understand, but which is hidden to 'prophane men' (line 22) or those he elsewhere calls the 'layetie' – see, for example, 'Valediction: forbidding mourning' (lines 7–8), and the whole argument of 'The Canonization' and 'The Extasie' – and any account of Donne's philosophy of love would have to note this idea, as well as taking account of the number of poems which begin and end in the pleasures of sexuality.

braver fine
the *Worthies* the Nine Worthies were nine great warriors, ranging from the legendary Hector of Troy in ancient times to the medieval Godfrey of Boulogne, who were occasionally brought on stage, as in Shakespeare's *Love's Labour's Lost* (V.2.), to boast of their great deeds. John Donne claims to exceed them both in achievement and in modesty
It were but madness ... / ... can finde none 'specular stone' was supposedly used in ancient times to build temples with transparent walls, but to be no longer available in John Donne's time; since there is none left to be cut, it would now be pointless to teach anyone the skill of doing so
Loves but their oldest clothes loves only the outward physical form, seen as the old clothes of the inner, spiritual self
though placed so although it is a love of this high and rare kind

THE SUNNE RISING

Poems in which lovers respond to the dawn, known as **aubades**, are very common; this is one of the most attractive of them, and one of the most popular of Donne's poems. In it he both celebrates a fulfilled and happy love, and develops further a favourite theme, of two lovers making up one world. Despite the poet's claims that the outer world is of no concern to him, he is evidently wide awake and alert; the poem suggests that he does not so much turn away from the world, as reach out to it, and bring it into the room he shares with his lover. For a fuller discussion, see Extended Commentaries where this poem is discussed in more detail.

Busie interfering

unruly disorderly

Must to thy motions lovers seasons run? must lovers adapt themselves to your time-keeping?

pedantique fussy, inclined to insist over-much on trivial matters (here, that it is morning)

sowre prentices ill-tempered apprentices

the King will ride King James was an enthusiastic huntsman, which obliged his attendants to get up early. The reference dates the poem as after 1603, when James came to the throne (and also, therefore, after John Donne's marriage in 1601)

Call countrey ants to harvest offices summon industrious farm labourers to the duties of harvesting

all alike unchanging

rags of time the usual divisions of time are seen as tattered clothing, in comparison with the timeless world of their love

reverend deserving respect

both the'India's of spice and Myne the East Indies (India) provided spices, the West Indies gold

play us imitate us

All honor's mimique; All wealth alchimie their love is the only true honour and wealth; all else is a false pretence (alchemy was the pseudo-science which tried to turn base metals into gold)

Thine age askes ease the sun, being so old, needs to lead an easier life than before

This bed thy center is, these walls, thy sphere this bed is the centre of the universe, and the walls of the room mark the new path of the sun's orbit around the centre

THE CANONIZATION

This is an elaborately argued poem in which the poet begins by suggesting that he and his lady are not important enough to deserve the world's critical attention, and asks to be left alone; he then changes his ground to claim that the perfection of their relationship will make them a model for future generations of lovers to copy. The first point is easier to make; the second is more difficult, if only because readers naturally dislike being told that the love they experience is of an inferior order.

John Donne was perhaps conscious of this difficulty himself: at any rate, the third stanza makes an awkward leap from comparing the lovers to insignificant and short-lived flies or moths, and then to the magical and self-renewing Phoenix, while the fourth seems to get held up on one idea, which (unusually for Donne) is repeated rather than developed. The two main lines of the poem's argument – the dismissal of the outside world, and the assertion of the central importance of the two lovers – echo those of 'The Sunne rising', and it is useful to compare the two in the light of the comment quoted earlier about Donne's 'irresistible rightness of tone'. How does the tone of the two poems compare? Is one more 'right' than the other, and if so, why?

The word 'love' is the chief **rhyming** word throughout the poem, used at the end of the first and last lines of each **stanza**.

Or ... or either ... or

chide mock

palsie physical shakiness associated with old age

Arts studies

Take you ... a place pursue a career, obtain a position at court

Observe ... his grace seek favour with some nobleman or bishop

the Kings reall ... / Contemplate either gaze at the King's real face (that is, seek to become a court favourite), or at the stamped face on his coins (that is, seek to acquire wealth)

what you will, approve do whatever you like

So so long as, provided that

my sighs in lines 10–15 John Donne mocks the sufferings experienced by the more conventional lovers in sixteenth-century poetry (sighs, fevers, tears)

a forward spring remove postpone an early spring

the plaguie Bill the weekly list of deaths from the plague in London

which quarrels move who provoke quarrels

Call her one ... / ... owne cost die in their mutual obsession they resemble the moths burned up in the candle flame they circle around, and the candles which gradually melt away. 'Die' was a **colloquial** term for orgasm, and it may that John Donne refers here to a somewhat depressing contemporary theory that each act of love-making reduces the length of life by a full day

the'Eagle and the Dove symbols of strength and gentleness, and also of aggression and submissiveness. The lovers unite qualities usually held to be opposites, or, developing the thought of the previous lines, they are each other's victims and oppressors

The Phœnix ridle the phoenix was a mythical bird. It was a riddle how it perpetuated its species, since there was never more than one bird at any time; it was believed to consume itself periodically in fire, and to rise renewed but unchanged from its own ashes

hath more wit / By us makes better sense because of us, is explained by us

one neutrall thing in the act of love-making they combine male and female, and so are, like the bird, sexually neutral

dye and rise the same see note on 'Call her one ...' above. Their love is unchanging before, during and after love making

prove / Mysterious become a mystery. Their unchanging passion puts them, like the phoenix or like the truths of religion, beyond the grasp of reason

unfit improper, unsuitable

if no peece of Chronicle wee prove even if our story will not be found in the history books

sonnets love **lyrics**

well wrought beautifully made (like a lyric)

becomes suits, is appropriate to

approve acknowledge

Canoniz'd made into saints. In Roman Catholic doctrine, men ask the saints to pray for them

invoke us call on us, pray to us

one anothers hermitage provided a spiritual refuge for each other

You ... that now is rage later lovers, who experience love only as a raging frustration, will recognise from the love lyrics that for John Donne and his mistress it was a condition of fulfilled peace

Who did the whole worlds soule contract ... / ... Courts two main **metaphors** are behind these highly compressed lines, as well as a **punning** shift in the meaning of 'glasses'. An alchemist extracts the essential quality of a substance by driving it through his apparatus into glass vessels or containers (the first metaphor); their passionate relationship has enabled them to extract the soul of the whole world, which is now held in the looking-glasses or mirrors of their eyes (the pun). What is actually reflected in their eyes is the image of the other, but as each is the whole world to the other (the second metaphor), this **image** epitomises, or represents in miniature form, the outer world of countries, towns and courts. Their eyes see and reflect, hence the reference to both 'mirrors' and 'spies'

Beg from above / A patterne of your love! ask heaven to grant us the blessing of a love like yours

SONG: SWEETEST LOVE, I DO NOT GOE

This is a simple but eloquent poem on the theme of parting, and another of the poems said in some manuscripts to have been written to fit an existing tune. The idea that separation is a kind of death is frequent in Donne's poems, as is the tender blackmail of the fourth **stanza,** suggesting that the woman's grief is unkind, and that she should become calm for his sake, if not for her own.

'tis best / ... fain'd deaths to dye to prepare myself for my real death by these simulated deaths of parting from you

sense feeling

come bad chance, / ... to'advance if misfortune comes we feed it by our own misery, and so allow it to gain a more complete and lasting hold on us

sigh'st my soule away in both Greek and Latin (both of which John Donne knew) the same word is used for both 'breath' and 'soul'

unkindly kinde her grief reveals her love, but it nonetheless causes him harm;

in thine my life thou waste in weakening herself in grief she weakens him as well

divining prophetic

Forethinke foresee, imagine. Compare 'Elegie: On his Mistris', lines 55–6, for the general thought

AIRE AND ANGELS

This is one of the most difficult of the *Songs and Sonets*, but it is also one of the finest, and deserves a rather fuller introductory note to set out the main lines of the poem's argument. Points of difficulty are discussed in the detailed notes which follow.

The starting point of the poem is the poet's sense that he loves, that is, he is aware that something has called his love into existence. But what does it mean to speak of 'my love'? This is the question to be answered in the poem.

The first six lines consider the idea that was put forward by some Italian theorists of love in the sixteenth century: that lovers in fact fall in love not with this or that individual person, but with a divine radiance which may be glimpsed shining through the human body (see the notes to lines 1–2 below for fuller comment on these ideas). This notion of a love which would be entirely spiritual is dismissed with laughter: such a love would be 'lovely' and 'glorious', but it would be the love of 'nothing'.

John Donne continues by granting that love comes from the soul; but just as his soul needed to inhabit his body before it could become real and active in this world (otherwise it could 'nothing doe'), so his love too must take on a body. This leads him to the second suggested answer to his question: that to speak of 'my love' is in fact to speak of the woman who is physically present before him. At first he accepts this as an answer ('I allow'). But her physical presence does not so much keep his love steady (as 'ballast' keeps a boat steady), as bewilder and overwhelm him with so much beauty: she is 'Extreme, and scatt'ring bright', perhaps the loveliest compliment ever paid in English poetry.

Neither of these two answers has proved satisfactory. Love is not simply a quality of the spirit, nor simply a quality of the body (it does not 'inhere' in either). But his love is real, and it does have an existence. For a final answer to his question he puts to new use an idea he had touched on earlier. An angel belongs to the realm of spirit, but to be known and recognised in this world it needs to inhabit some sort of body. This parallels the situation of his love. An angel, according to one medieval theory, takes on a body of air, which is the material element nearest to it in character and quality; accordingly, his love will adopt for its body the element of her love for him. (Donne uses the word 'sphere', on which see the note below.) This answer to Donne's question is not unlike the one arrived at in a very different mood in 'Loves Deitie':

It cannot bee

Love, till I love her, that loves mee.

It is her love for him that gives reality and existence to his love for her. The earliest opposition of spiritual and physical has been swept aside as both misleading and, in the last analysis, irrelevant.

> **Twice or thrice ... / ... thy face or name** some Christian thinkers in sixteenth-century Italy held that the true beauty of the body is only an outward sign of the moral and spiritual beauty of the soul, which itself radiates outwards from the absolute truth and beauty of God himself. Accordingly, they also held that the love of any beautiful woman was only a step towards love of the spiritual beauty she shared with all other beautiful women, and that in turn was only a step towards love of the Heavenly Beauty of God. In loving other women in the past, then, John Donne was loving an idea which is more fully revealed in her. For a similar idea, see 'The Good-morrow', lines 6–7
>
> **So in a voice ... / ... and worship'd bee** an angel which appears to man in the form of a voice or a flickering flame is only imperfectly revealed, just as the idea of an absolute beauty is only imperfectly revealed in the forms of individual women
>
> **Still** always
>
> **thou** the idea revealed through her
>
> **limmes** limbs
>
> **subtile** ethereal, intangible
>
> **assume** put on
>
> **wares** usually, the goods that might be carried on board a ship; here, her physical beauties, which 'sink' or overwhelm him
>
> **overfraught** overloaded
>
> **Ev'ry thy haire** each single hair
>
> **some fitter must be sought** some more suitable body for his love to take on
>
> **inhere** exist in, abide permanently in
>
> **aire, not pure as it, yet pure** an angel is a spirit, and therefore more pure than any material element, but air is also 'pure' in the sense that it is unmixed (and so not able to decay: for the idea, see the notes to 'The Good-morrow', line 19, 'What ever dyes ...')

spheare the main sense of the word here is 'element'. But John Donne also has in mind a second idea: each planet and star was believed to consist of a hollow sphere within which was a controlling Intelligence, that is, an angel. Her love is thus like a hollow sphere which encloses and holds his love, and his love is like the angel which guides and directs a star

Just such disparitie ... / ... will ever bee there is a disparity, or inequality, between the love of a man and the love of a woman, just as there is between the purity of an angel and the lesser purity of the air from which it forms its visible body.

These lines have caused much difficulty, since they seem to belittle women in general at the close of a poem which has at its centre a love and reverence for the one woman addressed. They have been interpreted as a poor joke; as the expression of a commonplace idea of John Donne's time; and as a way of filling out a complex stanza form after the poet had run out of ideas. None of these explanations is satisfactory. The solution seems to be that John Donne does not like to close a poem on an intense note, but prefers to withdraw a little, as if to allow the woman time to absorb and respond to what has been said. In this case the poem returns to the gentle but slightly teasing tone of the opening lines. For a poem with a similar pattern, compare 'Loves Growth'

THE ANNIVERSARIE

In this poem Donne meditates on the timelessness of the world of love, set against the world of time in which all human love necessarily takes place, and which is of course implied by the very idea of a poem celebrating the anniversary of their first meeting. It acknowledges the lover's need to use such words as 'forever', while recognising that in a world where men and women change, and die, we have no right to use these words; but the poet also knows that to brood on the inevitability of change is to destroy the possibility of love. In facing this paradox, and in exploring what it might be to love 'nobly', the poem can be seen as a sober and thoughtful treatment of the idea set out more extravagantly in 'The Sunne rising'. It is (for the present writer at least) one of the finest short poems in the language. It is discussed more fully in Extended Commentaries.

as they passe probably referring both to the Kings and their favourites, and to 'times'; the sun makes time, even as time, and all those subject to time, pass

his its (this was a normal usage in John Donne's time)

Two graves presumably they are not man and wife, and so will not be allowed to share a grave

dwells lives permanently

inmates temporary lodgers

prove / This ... there above experience this same, or perhaps an even greater love, in heaven

soules from their graves remove the body is seen as the grave of the soul, and death as the soul's release

throughly thoroughly, completely

wee ... all the rest in heaven all are fully blessed according to their capacity, so there can be no place for the sense of exceptional happiness they feel here in this world

nor of such subjects bee nor can be subjects of such Kings as themselves

refraine hold back, keep under control

love nobly their nobility will consist in their not being disturbed by either genuine or imaginary fears

till we attaine / To write threescore till we reach the sixtieth anniversary of our love

TWICKNAM GARDEN

This poem is a variation on a standard poetic theme, the contrast between the joys of spring and the miseries of the lover whose lady is unkind. Lucy, Countess of Bedford, lived with her husband at Twickenham (not far from London) from 1608 to 1617, during which time she was the patroness of Donne as well as of other poets. Much of the **imagery** of the poem is more traditional than usual with Donne – tears as the wine of love, for example – which is appropriate for the rather formal situation of the poem.

The last two lines provide a good example of Donne's gift for the succinct and emphatic statement of a strange or paradoxical idea; a number of later poets, notably Alexander Pope (1688–1744), were to base their poetic manner on this use of the **couplet**.

Blasted with sighs withered by the bitter air of his own sighs

surrounded flooded

balmes healing influences

else apart from his misery

selfe traytor one who betrays or harms himself

spider love spiders were popularly supposed to be full of poison

transubstantiates all transforms everything into another substance

Manna to gall that which should be sweet and nourishing is turned into something bitter and hurtful

the serpent alluding to the Old Testament story in which the devil, disguised as a serpent, tempted Eve to desire that which was forbidden (see Genesis 3)

'Twere wholesomer for mee it would be better for me

grave heavy, severe

Love let mee / ... of this place bee if he could he transformed into some unfeeling vegetable or statue, he could remain in the garden without being conscious either of his own pain or of its beauty, which seems to mock his feelings of misery

mandrake the mandrake plant was supposed to groan if uprooted (some manuscripts read 'grow' rather than 'groane')

Who's therefore true ... kills me she is unique among women in being faithful, but her fidelity (to someone else) is killing him with grief

LOVES GROWTH

In the first **stanza** Donne argues that love is not 'pure' but 'mixt', a compound of both sexual and spiritual feelings. The idea is stated in this summary way in line 14. But in the second stanza the tone deepens, and the summary gives way to the natural **imagery** which more profoundly suggests the real unity of the experience.

The questioning character of the poem is indicated by the use of such words as 'But', 'yet', 'though', all of which suggest a new turn in the thought. The natural imagery in the second stanza is less typical of Donne (though of course frequent in much other love poetry); but even here the suggestion of masculine arousal in 'loves awakened root', blending into the traditionally feminine notion of 'blossomes', is not simply decorative, but made to carry part of the poem's argument about the continuity between the spiritual and physical aspects of human love. This is also a poem which suggests Donne's capacity for tenderness as well as for masculine persuasiveness and energy; having begun the poem with the teasing suggestion that his love is liable to change, he then places her at the very centre of it with the eloquent line 'For, they are all concentrique unto thee' – where the word 'thee' seems to invite a longer than usual pause.

pure as usually in John Donne, not 'morally upright' but 'simple, unmixed', and therefore incapable of any change or decay

it doth endure / Vicissitude it does change and fluctuate – a teasing (and a loving) way to begin a poem which is going to conclude by asserting just the opposite of what is said here

which cures all sorrow / With more alluding to the medical theory that a disease was to be cured by the application of a like medicine

quintessence the essence of anything after all impurities were removed, thus isolating whatever was valuable and sustaining in it

paining soule, or sense as love is a compound, it can cause pain to both the body and the soul

working vigour strength and energy (including sexual energies)

abstract non-physical

as they use / To say ... their Muse as is generally said by those poets who are in love with poetry rather than with a woman. In Greek mythology the nine Muses presided over the various forms of the arts and sciences; here, as often, John Donne is mocking the conventional portrayal of love

elemented composed of a variety of elements

do act (compare line 19, 'Gentle love deeds')

And yet ... / ... but showne the stars are not made larger by the sun, but only made more visible by its light; so too their love will not be made greater by a new sexual element, but will only become more forcibly real to them (the stars were believed to reflect light from the sun)

If, as in water ... / ... take the suggestion is that the 'love deeds' would develop from their love as naturally and inevitably as the stirring of water produces a series of circles, each centred on the first movement

like so many spheares ... / ... unto thee their acts of love will all revolve around her, just as the various spheres which make up the heavens revolve around the earth

heate energy, especially sexual energy

in times of action in times of war

remit cancel

abate put an end to. The poem, which had begun by denying the infinity of love, concludes by asserting it

THE DREAME

This poem, like 'The Flea' or 'Twicknam Garden', is a variation on a standard poetic theme, in this case that of the poet's dream or daydream in which his mistress grants him what she has always refused in the waking world.

It is a good example of Donne's readiness to shift from one tone or mood to another in the course of a few lines; it begins tenderly ('Deare love, for nothing lesse than thee ...'), risks blasphemy (she is more than an Angel, since she can see into his heart), and ends, as often in Donne's work, with an attempted seduction (if she truly loves him, she will stay in his bed), with at least the hint of a sexual **pun** in the last words ('else would die').

It was a theame / ... for phantasie the subject matter of his dream was better suited to waking thought than to sleeping imagination

so truth ... / ... fables histories she is the essence of truth itself, so that even a thought of her turns dreams or stories into true histories

Tapers light candlelight

(For thou lovest truth) he is about to make a confession, and does so because he knows she would wish him to tell the truth

an Angell the sense becomes clear as the poem continues: at first he thought she was only an angel

beyond an Angels art angels were not believed to be able to read men's thoughts

it could not ... / Prophane it would necessarily be profane, or blasphemous

any thing but thee that is, anything less than herself, as, for example, a mere angel

show'd thee, thee proved your identity to me

as torches ... / ... put out a torch which had been lit briefly, and then put out, was easier to re-light than a fresh torch

THE DREAME continued

kindle set alight

goest to come go away intending to return later

A VALEDICTION: OF WEEPING

A valedictory poem is one bidding farewell. In this case Donne begins
with an elaborate defence of the his tears at parting, in which the tears
are treated as coins, emblems and globes or worlds. The ingenuity of
these **images** has been taken by some critics as evidence that Donne's
feelings were not deeply engaged, the assumption being that there is a
contradiction between intellectual complexity and genuine emotion.
Others have taken a contrary view, arguing that extremes of emotion are
easily translated into intellectual energy. Neither of these claims needs to
be taken as the expression of an absolute truth. The question for the
reader of Donne's poems is whether the effort required to unravel its
complexities is rewarded by something he or she can then find in the
poem.

In this case, it might be suggested that when the lady too begins to
weep (at line 17), the mood becomes more urgent. The beginning of the
third verse ('O more than Moone') suggests a sudden surge of emotion,
and like the last three words of the plea 'Weepe me not dead, in thine
armes' – the place above all others where he wants to remain, and where
he should be secure – demands to be read with feeling. The reader who
has found the poem oversubtle up to this point will then want to return
to see whether this urgency can be detected in the first lines too.

whil'st I stay here while I am still here

thy face ... / ... something worth the tears reflect her likeness, as a coin
carries the likeness of a ruler, and this gives them a value

Pregnant full

emblems of more an emblem is a picture with a symbolic content; the tear
carrying her likeness breaks on falling to the ground, which he interprets as
an **image** of how they too will be broken to 'nothing' when parted from each
other

on a divers shore in different countries, with the sea between them

make that ... *All* the plain globe is like a nought, or 'nothing'; when a map
is pasted on to it, it represents the world, or 'all'

So doth each teare / ... by that impression grow his blank tears become a world when they carry her image, because she is the world to him

thy teares my ... / ... heaven dissolved so as the lady (the poet's heaven) begins to weep she drowns all the little worlds that her image had made of his tears

O more than Moone ... / ... in thy spheare 'sphere' refers both to the range of power of a heavenly body (which would now be described as its gravitational field), and to her power over him. The moon has power over the tides, but she is more powerful, in that she draws forth seas of tears which destroy worlds

in thine armes the place above all others where he should be safe

forbeare / To teach do not teach

Since thou and I ... / ... the others death see the note on 'sigh'st my soule away', in 'Song: Sweetest love, I do not goe', line 26

Loves alchymie

This is the most savage of all the poems in which Donne denounces love. The title is explained by the final two lines: the lover is like a deluded alchemist who has sought in love the elixir which will cure all diseases and even prolong life, but he will have in the end to be content with whatever benefit is to be found in sexually entering a dead lump of mindless flesh; because that is the most one can expect of a woman. As in the previous poem, 'A Valediction: of Weeping', the comparisons are worked out in elaborate detail, but here there seems to be no question about the strength of feeling – though we should recognise even so that the starting-point for the poem need not have been an event in the poet's life. The poem is discussed more fully in the Extended Commentaries.

centrique central. There is a direct sexual reference in these first two lines

told counted

'tis imposture all it is all a cheat; love has no hidden mystery (contrast with this denial the entire argument of 'A Valediction: forbidding mourning')

as no chymique ... / ... or medcinall just as no alchemist ever found the elixir which would cure all diseases and prolong life, but was nonetheless delighted and encouraged if by chance he discovered something which smelled sweet, or had some medicinal value

a winter-seeming summers night love is as brief as a summer night, but as bleak and barren as a winter one (this is another good example of John Donne's use of the emphatic **couplet**)

our day our time of healthy life. See note to 'The Canonization', line 21

my man my servant. The suggestion is that love is a commonplace affair, and not a high spiritual state to be attained only by, a refined few

the short scorne of a Bridegroomes play the brief humiliation of the role of a bridegroom

Which he in her Angelique findes it is her mind which he finds angelic

that dayes rude hoarse minstralsey the crude and disagreeable music used at the wedding festivities

the spheares the harmonious movements of the various heavenly bodies were believed to produce a music too perfect to be heard by ordinary human ears

at their best / Sweetnesse and wit at their loveliest and cleverest

Mummy lumps of dead flesh. Dead bodies were sometimes preserved in bitumen for the sake of their supposed medicinal value

possest there are two meanings here: (a) sexually possessed; (b) inhabited by a demon or evil spirit, which gives the appearance of life to the 'Mummy'. The suggestion is that there may be some medicinal value in entering a woman's body, but not because of any meeting of the minds: all that is to be met there is the evil spirit which animates the body

A NOCTURNALL UPON S. LUCIES DAY

A nocturnal, or nocturne, is a work evoking the night (it is now most often used of a piece of music). There is some controversy as to the identity of the person to whom this poem refers. Whatever its background, it is a sombre and profoundly moving meditation on the sense of absolute loss. The poet feels both that his own life is exhausted, and that the world itself is dead; and whereas in 'The Canonization' he proposed that others would model their love on his, now he suggests that they should take his grief as an example.

The 'Nocturnall' is very different in argument from 'Loves Alchymie', but it is similarly relentless in tone, moving constantly back and forth between the words 'all' and 'nothing', and refusing to admit any possibility of recovery, unless the reference to her 'long nights festivall' carries with it a hint of her eventual resurrection.

S. Lucies day St Lucy's day, 13 December, was traditionally regarded as the Winter Solstice, or shortest day

spent exhausted

flasks the stars, which were supposed to store up energy from the sun, as flasks (cases of metal or horn) were used to store gunpowder

light squibs weak flashes

The generall balme sixteenth-century medical theory held that death and decay followed the using up of the 'balm' or life-giving natural essence which was contained in all living bodies

hydroptique suffering from dropsy and therefore afflicted with a raging thirst. All the life-giving forces in nature have been swallowed up by the diseased earth

Whither … life is shrunke life has shrunk down into the earth during the winter, as a dying man may be supposed to shrink down to the foot of the bed

enterr'd buried

Epitaph memorial inscription on a gravestone. His condition of grief is like a brief history or memorial of the general condition of lifelessness

In whom love … / … nothingnesse his love has extracted the very essence of nothingness, instead of the elixir of life usually sought by the alchemist

dull privations privation refers to the absence of something; dull privations would be those frustrations or disappointments which leave one feeling heavy and lifeless

ruin'd destroyed

re-begot re-born

All others … / … whence they beeing have human life ('beeing') depends on and is fed by the life-giving forces present throughout all created nature. John Donne alone is excluded from this source of being

limbecke alembic

Oft a flood … / … us two compare 'A Valediction: of Weeping', lines 14–18, and the notes to those lines

oft did we grow / … Care to ought else the world was supposed to have been created out of chaos. Whenever they showed concern for anything except each other the world of their love collapsed back into the condition of chaos

absences / ... made us carcasses physical separations in which however their souls remained united, so that their bodies were left as lifeless shells

Of the first nothing, the Elixer grown he has become not only the essence of nothing, but the essence of that first, original nothing which existed before the world began

I should preferre / ... some means even a beast is capable of making choices; he no longer is able to do so

Yea plants, yea stones detest in a sermon John Donne considers the possibility that even the stones may have life

All, all some properties invest every created thing has some characteristics

If I an ordinary nothing ... / ... be here an ordinary nothing is merely the absence of something, and thus, like the shadow, implies the existence or at least the possible existence of something. He however is 'None', an absolute nothing

my Sunne his lady

the Goat the sun enters the sign of the Goat (Capricorn) at the Winter Solstice, before the days begin to lengthen again

new lust the goat was considered the most lustful of animals. As the season changes to spring, all other lovers will feel their energies and desires restored

long nights festivall long sleep of death.

Let mee prepare towards her dedicate himself to her, contemplate the fact of her death, rather than the eventual return of the summer

Vigill to keep vigil is to sit up at night beside a dead body

Eve the evening before a saint's day or other church festival

THE APPARITION

In this poem Donne demonstrates his individuality by bringing together two conventional themes, both used in **Petrarchan** poetry: the rejected lover's complaint that his lady's chastity is killing him, and the warning that in old age she will long in vain for the pleasure she now refuses to grant him. The poem is characteristically shifting in tone, since the contempt he feels – or claims to feel – for the lady is made to co-exist, at the end of the poem, with an element of self-mockery; while he claims that his love is 'spent', or used up, the whole basis of the poem is of course his continuing but hopeless love for her. The poem is discussed more fully in the Extended Commentaries.

> **solicitation** entreaty, pleading
>
> **fain'd vestall** the lady has falsely claimed to be dedicated to preserving her virginity (priestesses at the Roman temple of Vesta swore an oath of virginity)
>
> **winke** flicker, as if about to go out
>
> **whose thou art then** the lover who will possess you at that time
>
> **Aspen** trembling, as the tree of the same name does in even a slight breeze
>
> **quicksilver** mercury, a metal which has a semi-liquid form, and in small quantities could seem to resemble beads of sweat
>
> **A veryer ghost than I** even more a ghost than I shall be
>
> **What I will say ... / ... still innocent** if he makes her so afraid with his threats that she decides to remain chaste after his death, he will not have the satisfaction of seeing her suffer in the way that he predicts
>
> **spent** finished, exhausted

A VALEDICTION: FORBIDDING MOURNING

In his *Life of Dr John Donne*, Izaac Walton says that Donne gave this poem to his wife before leaving to travel in France, Germany and Belgium in 1611. Modern editors have been inclined to doubt this claim, which was not made until the fourth edition of Walton's work (first edition 1640; fourth edition 1675). Whatever the reality behind the story, the intensity of feeling in the poem is remarkable; consider, as one example, the way the word 'must' in line 22 ('Though I must goe') seems to push itself forward, pleading for her to accept the inevitable fact, although formally the stresses fall on 'I' and 'goe'.

The compass **image** at the end of the poem has often been discussed as an example of the '**conceit**', that is, a comparison of two or more ideas apparently unlike, which is only gradually revealed to be justified – in this case, comparing parted lovers and a pair of compasses. In this example, it might be suggested that the conceit is both apt – though they are separated while he is travelling abroad, the two lovers are also essentially united – and inadequate (see the note on the last line of the poem, which also offers a defence of the way the comparison seems to break down).

But there are other moments in the poem which seem immediately natural and convincing: for example, even as Donne suggests that the two can rise above the sadness of a physical separation, he lingers on eyes, lips and hands, as if enacting the last gaze, kiss and wave of parting lovers – just the features which make the experience so stressful. Despite the elaborate comparisons and **analogies**, the poet cannot deny that their separation will be acutely painful, and that there is no argument which can take away the pain.

teare-floods ... sigh-tempests the conventional expressions of grief

move cause

T'were prophanation ... / ... the layetie our love those ordinary men and women who have not been (as they have) inititiated into the secrets of love

Moving of th'earth ... / ... is innocent the contrast is between obvious occasional movements of the earth, such as earthquakes, which leave men counting the cost of the damage done and anxious about what possibly worse disaster such an event may foreshadow, and the continual trembling movement which was believed to run through the whole universe, but which passed unnoticed, neither causing nor foretelling any harm. It is of course to this second kind of movement that the lovers' feeling are compared

sublunary changeable

(Whose soule is sense) the essence of whose love is physical

admit allow

elemented it composed it. A predominantly physical love cannot survive physical separation

so much refin'd / ... what it is a favourite idea in John Donne's poetry. Their love has reached that high level at which it becomes a mystery of which even they themselves cannot give an account. Compare 'The Extasie', lines 21–2

Inter-assured mutually confident

endure not yet / A breach nonetheless do not suffer a break

gold to ayery thinnesse beate gold is beaten out to make gold leaf

compasses instrument used for drawing circles

as that comes home as the two legs of the compass are closed after use

firmnes literally, the physical stiffness of the leg of the compass; in terms of the **conceit**, the moral strength he is urging on her throughout the poem

drawes my circle just makes me complete a perfect circle: that is, gives a point and direction to my journey

makes me end, where I begunne logically the compass **analogy** breaks down here. The lady is now thought of as both (a) the point on the circumference of the circle where he started, and to which he returns in completing the circle, and as (b) the centre, the still point around which he revolves. This is not so much a slip as a sign of the pressure of feeling in the poem; the reality is that their parting feels like a death (as the first verse suggests), and the attempt to prove otherwise is bound to fail

THE EXSTASIE

This has been one of the most discussed of John Donne's poems. It may be divided into three sections. The first of these (lines 1–20) describes the situation, in which the souls of the two lovers go out from their bodies (this is the literal meaning of 'ecstasy'). The second section (lines 21–48) employs the device of an imaginary listener and observer, in order to summarise what is communicated between the two souls. The last part of the poem puts forward reasons for the souls to return to their bodies: among these are the desirability of sexual love, and the duty to 'reveal' love to those who would be too 'weak' to believe in love without some such sign. The logical development, then, is through a sense of the ecstatic union of souls to an admission of the claims of the body, and thence to an attempt at a fuller understanding of the relation between body and soul in love.

The chief difficulty of the poem, perhaps, is that while it argues for wholeness, it does so in ways which continually suggest the opposition of soul and body, or the superiority of the spiritual over the physical: notice the suggestion of an unfortunate necessity in the lines, 'So *must* pure lovers soules descend / T'affections' – emphasis added, as if the world of ordinary human feeling and expression was inferior to the dialogue of two disembodied souls.

The poem is sometimes printed as a series of **quatrains**, sometimes as a continuous piece of **verse**.

The violets the violet was traditionally associated with faithful love

fast balme the warm moisture that holds them fast together

Our eye-beames twisted one theory of sight held that it was caused by the contact of a beam sent out from the eye with the object seen. Their eye-beams are twisted because they are looking at each other

to'entergraft a gardener produces a graft by inserting a shoot into a slit made in another plant, so that the sap can circulate through both freely. Their fingers are twined together, as if the same 'balm' flowed through both of them

to get to beget, to create

As 'twixt two equall Armies ... / ... her, and mee the uncertain outcome of a battle was sometimes represented by artists by a pair of scales hung ('suspended') between the two armies. Here the bodies are like the opposed armies, while the souls are sent out, like envoys, to 'negotiate' between them

sepulchrall statues statues on tombs

a new concoction the process of refining metals and minerals by heat. The observer will be even more 'refined' after he has heard them

unperplex resolve their difficulties

Wee see, we saw not what did move in their state of ecstasy, or separation from their bodies, they realise that they had not previously understood what attracted them to each other

Mixture of things, they know not what the soul was presumed to be a mixture of things because it had to perform many different functions. It was a common idea that we are unaware of the nature of our own souls

Love ... doth mixe againe love further mixes these souls, which are already a mixture of things

both one, each this and that see 'The Good-morrow', note to line 14 ('Let us possess ...'), for this idea of one person made out of two

When love ... / ... two soules when love so combines two separate souls that they become one new soul. Compare 'entergraft' in line 9

Defects of lonelinesse controules the two souls united together are stronger than either was separately, because each can remedy the weaknesses or 'defects' of the other

Atomies atoms

soules, whom no change can invade the soul, unlike the body, was not obliged to suffer change. Their ecstasy has shown them that their love exists on the level of the soul rather than on the level of the body, and consequently their love too is free from change. See 'A Valediction: forbidding mourning', lines 13–16, and the notes on these lines

forbeare avoid, keep away from

Wee are / The'intelligences, they the spheares they are related to their bodies just as an angel is related to the sphere it controls. See 'Aire and Angels', line 25 and note

Yeelded their forces, sense, to us the natural forces of the body are the powers of the senses. They have been able to achieve their state of ecstasy because their bodies temporarily gave up these powers

Nor are drosse to us in some accounts of love, the body was seen as impure matter to be left behind or discarded. John Donne here, as usually, rejects this view

allay alloy, that is, a base metal mixed in with one of a higher value. John Donne's distinction between dross and alloy is a slight one: on the one hand the body is not to be rejected, but on the other it acknowledged as the inferior element in the body-soul partnership. The line is perhaps not very satisfactory

On man ... / ... to body first repaire the planets and stars can only influence man by first affecting the air. Sometimes, therefore, a spiritual force requires a physical medium through which to work; in the same way, the spiritual union of their souls may require the physical union of their bodies

repaire goes to

As our blood ... / ... which makes us man the idea here comes from contemporary theories of physiology. Since we are made of the two dissimilar components, body and soul, it was held that there must be a link connecting the two; this link was the vapour, or spirit, produced by the blood

need are needed

subtile there are two meanings here: (a) ethereal, impalpable; (b) complex (compare modern usages of the word 'fine')

affections passions

faculties powers of action

Which sense ... apprehend that are within the range of the senses

Else a great Prince in prison lies the loving self is only made free if body and soul work together in the harmony described in lines 61–7

that so / Weake men ... / ... the body is his booke see the note introducing this poem, and 'Elegie: To his Mistris going to Bed', lines 40–3, and notes

dialogue of one see line 26 of the poem

Let him still mark us ... / ... to bodies gone he will realise how little their love is altered by the return of their souls to their bodies. Until this point, the bystander has been listening; the change to a bystander who watches the couple making love, in effect a voyeur, provides an awkward close to the poem

LOVES DEITIE

This is a rather formal poem, based on the idea of a 'golden age' in which love was given and accepted freely, and the God of Love did not have the power to make anyone fall hopelessly and unsuccessfully in love, as the poet has now done. But having seemed to suggest that he has experienced the worst pain the God of Love can inflict, Donne characteristically complicates the poem in the last verse; the woman he loves could only come to love him by betraying the man she already loves, and to see that would be even more painful than to endure her rejection of him.

before the god of Love was borne that is, in the days when love could be offered and enjoyed in total freedom

hee, who then lov'd most even the greatest lover of those days

produc'd a destinie appointed a special fate for lovers

that vice-nature, custome, lets it be as we grow accustomed to our destiny, and it becomes second nature to us, we no longer try to resist it

meant not so much did not intend love to have so much authority and power

even equal

His office ... / Actives to passives it was his task obligingly to pair up men and women (those who make the advances, and those who accept them)

Correspondencie / Only his subject was his only business was to ensure a perfect and equal match

prerogative right of authority

Jove Jupiter, the greatest of the ancient Roman gods

To rage ... / ... God of Love the God of Love now claims new rights, and dictates the feelings and actions of unhappy and frustrated lovers as well

ungod rebel against, overthrow

child Cupid, the God of Love, is usually represented as a winged child armed with a bow and arrows

murmure complain

loves before already has a lover

Falshood is worse ... / ... should love mee she would have to be false to her present lover in order to love the poet; rather than see her turn false, he would prefer that she continue to hate him

THE WILL

This is another rather formal poem in which, unusually for Donne, each **verse** has a kind of **refrain** (in the last three lines). The lady to whom he offered his love did not value it as he thought she ought to, and he is now about to die because she has rejected him; therefore he proposes to leave his various qualities and possessions to those who are least likely to value them properly. The poem makes a number of **satirical** hits, usually at rather obvious targets, but the tone of the poem also implies a satirical view of the poet himself, particularly in the suggestion in the last verse that he will 'undoe' the world by dying – in reality the world will, of course, continue on its way without him.

Argus in Greek mythology, a giant with a hundred eyes

If they be blinde the God of Love is often represented blindfolded

Fame rumour, gossip

who'had twenty more twenty more lovers

the planets planets were sometimes known as wandering stars, and so were supposed incapable of constancy

ingenuity ingenuousness, frankness

Jesuites members of the Roman Catholic Society of Jesus, an extremely active Catholic group which had been founded by Ignatius Loyola (1491–1556) in 1534. The common complaint against the Jesuits in John Donne's day was their defence of equivocation, the use of ambiguous words so as to conceal a true meaning (John Donne himself was probably educated by Jesuits)

Buffones fools, clowns

My silence ... hath beene a stock joke against travellers who told improbable tales of things seen and done on their voyages

Capuchin member of a monastic order vowed to absolute poverty

My faith ... / Of Amsterdam Roman Catholic teaching argued that salvation depended on good works as well as faith. The Schismatics were their logical opposites, an extreme Puritan group who believed that salvation depended on faith alone

Courtship civility, courtliness of manner. The implication is that scholars are generally lacking in any elegance of manners

bare naked

gamesters gamblers

that holds my love disparity who considers his love beneath her dignity, not worth having

Mine industrie to foes he owes his hard work to the opponents against whom he had to defend himself

Schoolmen medieval theologians, whose endlessly subtle arguments led to doubt and uncertainty

excesse sickness was supposed to result from the excess of some element in the constitution

my wit his cleverness

the passing bell the church bell rung to announce someone's death

physick bookes medical books

writen rowles / Of Morall counsels documents full of good advice

Bedlam the London lunatic asylum

My brazen medals ancient bronze coins, no longer in use as currency, and so useless to the starving

dost my gifts thus disproportion she claims to have no use for the things he is able to offer her

undoe ruin, defeat

all your beauties will bee no more worth her beauty is only precious so long as she has someone to admire it

who doth neglect both mee and thee it is hard to see how a lady with twenty lovers (1.8) can be accused of neglecting the God of Love. Perhaps she has refused all the others as well, or perhaps he feels his love is the only true one; lovers, especially poetic lovers, are inclined to be egotistic

practise put into practice

three poet, lady and Love himself

THE RELIQUE

The poet argues that the true miracle of his love for the lady of the poem, even though it may never be understood, is that it is a love not based on sexual desire. It is another of the poems in which John Donne writes of human love as a mystery, that is, something beyond the reach of our understanding, and at its highest levels attainable by only a few exceptional individuals. This idea is put forward seriously in the poem, but the sexual knowingness of lines 3–4 is not quite consistent with a whole-hearted celebration of entirely spiritual love; see too the note on lines 29–30, where Donne suggests that the laws which have restricted sexual freedom are a kind of injury.

The poet and critic T.S. Eliot, one of those who argued for Donne's importance as a poet, singled out the line 'a bracelet of bright hair about the bone' for special praise; it has Donne's characteristic intellectual precision, in this case combined with a remarkable visual immediacy.

Relique a relic is a part of the body or belongings of a holy person, kept after his or her death as an object of reverence. The worship of relics had been abandoned by the Reformed churches in John Donne's day

When my grave ... / ... entertaine this practice was not uncommon until quite recent times

that woman-head that womanly nature. The sexual reference of these lines is re-inforced by the similarity of 'woman head' to 'maidenhead'

device trick. At the Day of Resurrection (the 'last busie day') our souls will have to travel the earth to gather our scattered bodily members. The trick therefore is to put a part of each lover in the same grave, so that they will be able to meet again briefly even on the very last day

fall happen

Where mis-devotion doth command where false worship, as of relics, is still practised

a Mary Magdalen the bright hair round his wrist will suggest St Mary Magdalen to the grave-digger, because she was always represented in art with long golden hair (she was identified with the 'sinner' who washed Christ's feet with her hair: see the Bible, Luke 7)

A something else probably a dismissive phrase: he will be supposed one of her lovers, to whom she gave the hair as a token before her reform

thereby by the decision of the King and the Bishop

at such time at such periods of mistaken belief

knew not what wee lov'd, nor why compare 'A Valediction: forbidding mourning', lines 17–18

Difference of sex ... / ... Angells doe similar to angels who have no sexual nature, their love had no sexual element

meales the kiss is seen as the food of the soul

the seales / ... sets free the restrictions on human love-making, which do not belong to Nature, but are the consequences of relatively recent man-made laws and conventions. The word 'injur'd' suggests that the poet is not completely convinced that the absence of any sexual element in their love is an unmixed good

These miracles wee did i.e., not the miracles that an age of 'mis-devotion' will attribute to them, but the nonetheless genuine miracle of an exceptional love

THE EXPIRATION

This short poem is based on an idea which also appears in 'Song: Sweetest love, I do not goe', that the soul is in the breath, and on the thought to which Donne returns often, that parting resembles death.

While this is a relatively simple poem, it is worth noting that the **rhyme** scheme allows both verses to end with the word 'go', which also begins the second verse; the first verse begins with the word 'So', which reappears in the rhyme so / go at the end. In this way the sense of the inevitability of their parting literally echoes through the poem.

vapors causes to evaporate

benight turn into night

We ask'd none leave ... / ... as saying, Goe they did not ask anyone for permission to love, nor will they allow anyone the power to destroy them simply by ordering them to part

Except unless

Being doubled dead since I am already dead twice over

going, and bidding, goe leaving her, and telling her to leave him

HOLY SONNETS: DIVINE MEDITATIONS

For a comment on the tradition of meditation, see the section 'Reading the *Divine Poems*'. Meditation was widely practised throughout the sixteenth and seventeenth centuries, but it was especially favoured by the Jesuits, and it is likely that Donne was introduced to the practice by his early teachers (the *Spiritual Exercises* devised by the Jesuit Ignatius Loyola received papal approval in 1548).

In this sequence of six sonnets, Donne meditates on two related themes: personal sinfulness, and the judgement of God on sinners.

AS DUE BY MANY TITLES

The argument of the poem is that Donne belongs to God by right, since God both created him, and (through Christ) died for him; but in his despair he feels that he has been abandoned by God, and only the Devil seeks him.

titles legal rights

resigne surrender

decay'd corrupted by sin

blood see note on 'whose paines ... repaid' below

thy sonne ... to shine playing upon 'son' and 'sun'. The believing Christian is 'the child of God'; according to the biblical promise, the 'righteous' will 'shine forth' like the 'sun' at the end of the world (see Matthew 13:43)

whose paines ... repaid Christ's sufferings on the Cross were seen as the payment of a ransom, freeing those who held to the Christian faith from the pains they would otherwise have had to endure in hell

Thy sheepe God's love for mankind is often compared in the Bible to that of the shepherd for his sheep

thine Image in the biblical account, 'God created man in his own image' (see Genesis 1:27)

a temple of thy Spirit divine according to Christian teaching, the Holy Spirit dwells in all Christian believers, who may thus be said to resemble temples

usurpe in mee unjustly claim possession of me (compare the first line of the poem)

that's thy right that which rightly belongs to God

Except unless

OH MY BLACKE SOULE!

This poem is a prayer for the grace without which the poet cannot be truly repentant of his sins. The theological paradox Donne addresses is that it is only through God's loving care, freely given, that the sinful human can recognise the need to seek God's forgiveness. The poem is thus concerned with the large questions of free will that were at the centre of much religious controversy in the period.

> **summoned / By sicknesse ... champion** the reference is to a joust or tournament, where the herald summoned two rivals to combat; a champion was one who fought for or on behalf of someone else
>
> **durst not turne** does not dare to return
>
> **deaths doome** the sentence of death
>
> **damn'd** condemned
>
> **hal'd** dragged
>
> **Yet grace ... / ... grace to beginne** in line 9 'grace' is the mercy of God, which would not be denied to those who truly repented; in line 10 it refers to the state of mind in which the need for repentance is admitted, and which could only come about as the result of God's prompting
>
> **might** power, property
>
> **white** white was the colour of innocence

THIS IS MY PLAYES LAST SCENE

In this poem Donne imagines that he is on his deathbed preparing to meet God's judgement. It is useful to compare this poem with the preparations Donne did in fact make for his death in 1631 (see Background). In his sermons Donne explored in detail the relation between a person's death, and the judgement that was made then by God, and the general judgement that would be made on all men and women at the end of the world.

> **My spans last inch** a span is a small distance, or brief length of time
>
> **unjoynt** separate (in this case literally, as the body's joints fall apart after death)
>
> **I shall sleepe ... / ... my ever-waking part** in these lines 'I' is the body, and the 'ever-waking part' is the soul. John Donne believed that the soul was judged at the very instant of death, while the resurrection of the body had to wait until the final Day of Judgement (compare 'The Relique', lines 8–11)
>
> **that all may have their right** his soul will go to its proper home in heaven,

and his body will return to the earth (according to biblical teaching, God made the first man from the dust); it is, therefore, only fitting that his sins should go to their natural home in hell

and would presse me his sins want to thrust him into hell

Impute me righteous for this important idea, see the note on 'imputed grace' in the elegy 'To his Mistris Going to Bed', line 42

AT THE ROUND EARTHS IMAGIN'D CORNERS

In this poem Donne imagines the Day of Judgement, and begs for time to be allowed for him to repent his sins. The opening of the poem, which creates a powerful visual **image** of the end of the world (a subject which was often treated by religious painters in the period), is a good example of the use of the imagination to help concentrate the mind while meditating.

At the round earths imagin'd corners the idea of the 'four corners of the earth' comes from the Bible (see Revelation 7:1); John Donne knew from the work of sixteenth-century astronomers that the world was in fact round, and therefore of course had no corners

scattred bodies the parts of the body scattered over the earth as dust and bones (see note on 'I shall sleepe ...' in 'This is my playes last scene', lines 6–7)

flood ... fire according to the biblical stories, God had destroyed the world by flood in the time of Noah, and would finally destroy it by, among other things, fire (see Genesis chapters 6 to 9, and Revelation 6 and the following chapters)

never tast deaths woe Christ had promised that some of those who heard him speak would never 'taste of death' (see Matthew 16:28)

But let them sleepe that is, delay the Day of Judgement

'Tis late it will be too late

Teach mee how to repent see 'Oh my blacke Soule!', lines 9–10

seal'd my pardon Christ's death on the Cross purchased an offer of pardon for mankind in general; if John Donne learns how to repent his sins, his particular pardon will be confirmed or authorised

IF POYSONOUS MINERALLS

In this **sonnet** Donne asks God to forget his sins, and so allow him to escape the damnation he has deserved. The paradox that underlies the poem is that the human capacity to reason raises mankind above the beasts, but also makes possible the idea of sin, which comes from disobedience. But even in exploring this paradox, Donne recognises that he might be misusing his reason, by seeming to challenge God's wisdom, and in the last six lines of the poem he turns from argument to prayer.

> **If that tree / ... else immortall us** death came into the world when Adam and Eve ate the fruit of the tree of the knowledge of good and evil, which God had forbidden (see Genesis 3)
>
> **Cannot be damn'd** only creatures capable of a reasoned choice were liable to damnation (see above)
>
> **And mercy ... / ... why threatens hee?** why does God angrily threaten eternal punishment when it is easy for him to show mercy, and when to do so increases his glory?
>
> **thine onely worthy blood** only the blood of Christ, shed at the Crucifixion, is able to drown the memory of the poet's sins
>
> **Lethean flood** in ancient Greek mythology the souls of the dead drank from the river Lethe, whose water had the power of drowning all memory of an earlier existence on earth
>
> **That thou remember ... if thou wilt forget** some people ask God to remember and forgive their sins in terms of a claim on his mercy, since their pardon had been bought by the death of Christ. The poet prefers to hope that God will simply forget his sins (see Jeremiah 31:34)

DEATH BE NOT PROUD

The argument of the poem is that Death is not all-powerful, since it must eventually give way to eternal life; what we fear as death is (for the Christian believer) only a form of sleep, from which we shall awake at the Day of Judgement, when Death will be abolished.

> **From rest and sleepe ... / ... much more must flow** since so much pleasure results from rest and sleep, which are only as pictures of death, even more pleasure must result from death itself
>
> **Rest ... deliverie** death provides a rest for man's body, and a birth or liberation for his soul
>
> **poppie** the juice of the poppy is a narcotic
>
> **And better than thy stroake** the sleep brought on by drugs is heavier and more refreshing than that of death. The idea evidently conflicts with lines

5–6 above, which suggests that we will gain more pleasure from the sleep of death

why swell'st thou then? why do you swell up with pride?

Death thou shalt die the idea of Death as an enemy to be destroyed comes from the Bible (see 1 Corinthians 15:26, 54–5)

Batter my heart

The poem is a plea for God to enter and take over the poet's life, thus saving him from the power of Satan. It develops through three main **images**. The first is that of a potter or craftsman repairing a damaged vessel, and has behind it the idea of God as the creator. The next two images both explain Donne's sinful nature by comparing him to the victim of a violent assault: first in military terms (he is like a town, which has been briefly captured and ruled by the enemy), and then in sexual terms (he is like a woman compelled to marry against her will). In each case Donne suggests that God must act in a similarly violent manner to save him, by retaking the town, or by ravishing the woman, and thus cancelling the wrong marriage.

The literalness with which these images of assault are developed is undoubtedly dramatic, but perhaps leaves the modern reader feeling uncomfortable. The idea that the Christian Church can be seen as the Bride of Christ comes from the Bible, but Donne's image makes Christ a ravisher, not just a husband. It is as if Donne feels that an image which is strong enough for other men and women is not powerful enough for him: others can be wooed into salvation, but Donne must be taken by force.

The paradox which drives the poem on is however a profound one. On the one hand, Donne wishes to surrender himself entirely to God; on the other, he needs to feel that the self claimed by God is still the unique Donne. The poem is both a total surrender to an all-powerful God, and – through its extraordinary verbal energy, as in the very first line – an assertion of Donne's personality. The same paradox is found in a later poem, 'A Hymne to God the Father'.

The question which causes Donne so much concern has in fact often been raised in discussions of the nature of Heaven in a more general form: in what sense will the person who is saved, and granted eternal life in Heaven, still be the person he or she was in this life?

Perhaps its best known appearance in this form is in *In Memoriam*, by Alfred, Lord Tennyson, published in 1850, where Tennyson wonders whether he will continue to enjoy in an afterlife the friendships that he has formed during his lifetime on earth. The huge popular success of *In Memoriam* suggests that this is an issue which many Christian readers felt relevant to their lives, but it was clearly one which Donne felt with great intensity.

> **three-person'd God** the Holy Trinity (God the Father, God the Son and God the Holy Spirit)
>
> **shine** polish
>
> **bend** direct, apply
>
> **to'another due** owing duty and obedience to another (see 'As due by many titles', lines 1 -2, and note to those lines)
>
> **to no end** unsuccessfully
>
> **Reason your viceroy ... should defend** his reason should rule him in God's name and on God's behalf
>
> **and would be lov'd faine** the poet wishes to be loved by God
>
> **untie, or breake that knot againe** that is, the 'knot' which is said to bind together the partners in a marriage
>
> **enthrall mee** make a slave of me
>
> **except you ravish mee** unless you rape me

SINCE SHE WHOM I LOV'D

John Donne's wife Ann died in August 1617, a few days after giving birth to a stillborn child. Throughout the poem Donne tries to persuade himself that her death was in accordance with divine justice and mercy, but at the same time, and often in the same words, the poem expresses his sense of injustice. It is the tension between the two ideas that gives the **sonnet** its terrific force.

'Since she whom I lov'd' can usefully be read alongside 'Batter my heart'. In that poem Donne asks God to 'ravish' him, that is, to take over his life completely. In this poem, God has instead ravished Donne's wife, that is, taken her from this life and into heaven. Donne has to accept that in a sense his prayer has been answered by her death, because now his attachment to this life has been weakened, and his thoughts have been turned towards heaven.

But he cannot help feeling that his love for his wife taught him how to love, and thus led him towards God, not away from Him (see lines 5–6); God's action in taking her has been unnecessarily harsh. So, in line 3, Donne describes her as having been taken 'early into heaven': since heaven is our goal, it cannot be bad to arrive there early, and yet – since she was still young – the phrase also suggests that she has been taken from him *too* early. Similarly, in line 4, Donne says that his mind is now concentrated 'Wholly on heavenly things'; it must be good that this is true, since the Christian believer should constantly be aware of matters of faith, but the phrase also suggests that this world has now been left meaningless to him.

This is a difficult poem, not because there are some local obscurities (these are discussed in the notes which follow), but because the situation of which it tries to give an account is so painful. It can be represented in a simplified form by the image of the Christian believer grieving by a graveside, and struggling to say 'Thy will be done' – the proper Christian response – and at the same time to give full weight to the human feelings of loss, anger and confusion which are necessarily aroused by the early death of a loved wife.

her last debt / To Nature the idea that we all 'owe' Nature a death was more or less **proverbial**

and to hers, and my good is dead the **syntax** of this line is uncertain. Either (a) his wife's death means that she can no longer do anything for her own or for her husband's good; or (b) her death has been for her good (she is now in heaven) and for his (since her death he thinks only of heaven). The first reading offers only the bleak facts, and provides no comfort; the second offers comfort only to a man whose faith is still more powerful than his grief. As is suggested above, both meanings may be present in the poem

early Ann Donne was only thirty-three when she died; the implication of the line is that she died too early

ravished caught up from the earth; the word suggests both violence and the act of love

Here here on earth

whett encourage

so streames do shew the head just as a stream can be traced back to its source, so all human loves can be traced back to their source, which is to be found in the love of God. See 'Aire and Angels', lines 1–2, and the note to those lines

A holy thirsty dropsy a reverent but immoderate desire. The sense is that John Donne's thirst for God's love has been fed, but he can never feel that it has been fed enough; the thirst is 'holy' because it is not a sin to desire God's love, but it is also diseased (a 'dropsy') because he remains endlessly unsatisfied

when as thou / … offring all thine God now offers John Donne his divine love in exchange for the human love of which he was deprived with the death of his wife

But in thy tender jealousy … / … putt thee out John Donne interprets God's treatment of him as that of a jealous and possessive lover. God's jealousy is shown in two ways: firstly, he has removed John Donne's wife (his 'saint and Angel'), fearing that John Donne might love her too much; and secondly, he has ensured that none of John Donne's love would be wasted on the pleasures of this world, by providing for him a life of pain and disappointment

GOOD FRIDAY, 1613. RIDING WESTWARD

On Good Friday, 1613, Donne was travelling westwards to visit friends, and it was presumably on or shortly after this journey that he composed this poem. The argument is in three stages. At first Donne admits that at this time, Good Friday, he should be facing the East, looking towards the place of Christ's death on the Cross (lines 1–14). However, even Nature could not endure the sad spectacle of the dead Christ and the weeping Mary, and for Donne too the sight would be unbearable (lines 15–32). But although he rides away, the **image** of the Crucifixion is present to his mind; his back is turned only to receive punishment for his sins, and when he has been sufficiently punished, Christ will acknowledge him, and then at last Donne can turn to face Christ.

Let mans Soule … / … devotion is a man's soul is moved by devotion to God, as a sphere is guided by the Intelligence or angel within it. See 'Aire and Angels', line 25, and note

And as the other Spheares … / … whirld by it according to sixteenth-century scientists, the natural motion of the spheres which composed the universe was from West to East, but a number of cosmic forces hindered or deflected this movement, including what was known as the Primum Mobile or 'first mover'

Hence is't ... / ... toward the East his journey carries him physically towards the West, while his devotion compels his soul towards the East

a Sunne ... / ... endlesse day beget there is a play here on 'sun' and 'son' (Christ, the Son of God). Christ was raised on the Cross, and endured death ('set'); this sacrifice made eternal life ('endlesse day') available to those who adopted the Christian faith

of too much weight for mee too great for me to bear

Who sees Gods face ... must dye so God told Moses in the Bible (see Exodus 33:20)

that is selfe life that is the principle of life

Lieutenant deputy

shrinke withdraw in horror. Matthew's gospel records the disturbances in nature at the moment of Christ's death (see Matthew 27:51–3)

footstoole the earth is described as God's footstool in the Bible (see Isaiah 66:1)

the Sunne winke during the Crucifixion 'there was darkness over all the land' for three hours (see Matthew 27:45)

tune all spheares at once the different sounds made by the movement of the spheres which made up the universe was made were supposed to produce a perfect harmony

Zenith ... Antipodes God is the highest point ('endlesse height') both to us and to those on the other side of the world

that blood ... / ... of all our Soules the soul was sometimes held to reside, or be seated, in the blood; in fact, John Donne argues, all our souls are supported by the blood shed in Christ's self-sacrifice

if not of his whether or not Christ's soul resided in his blood

Make durt of dust change dry dust into moist dirt

rag'd make ragged

Gods partner here Christ was the child of Mary as well as of God

from mine eye not present before his eyes

the tree the Cross

Corrections punishments which will correct his conduct

Restore thine Image man was originally made in the image or likeness of God, but this resemblance was destroyed by man's sin. John Donne asks to be restored to this original likeness, and so made fit to face Christ

A HYMNE TO CHRIST

The occasion of this moving poem was Donne's voyage to Germany in 1619, when he was chaplain to a diplomatic mission; nearing fifty years of age, and in poor spirits, Donne did not expect to return from the journey. The poem is essentially a preparation for death, reminiscent in mood of 'A Nocturnall upon S. Lucies Day'. The image here of God as a demanding and jealous lover, from whom nonetheless Donne seeks still more signs of love, recalls the last eight lines of the **sonnet** on the death of his wife two years earlier.

The fact that 'A Hymne to Christ' can stand comparison with these poems is a measure of its greatness. If in the sonnet 'Since she whome I lov'd' Donne tries to reconcile acceptance of God's will with his own natural human grief, here he tries to transform a weary willingness to die – which comes close to despair, and therefore to being a sin – into an acceptance of whatever God chooses to bring. The opening lines of the second verse are remarkable other poets might have offered up their lives as a sacrifice to God, and in doing so recognised that they were accepting the loss of those whom they loved ('all whom I lov'd there'), but it is hard to think of another poet who would do as Donne does here, and go on to accept their loss of him ('and who lov'd mee') – including, we must suppose, his seven surviving children. It is entirely characteristic of Donne to examine closely in this way an idea which others might have been content to leave unexplored.

> **thy Arke** the ark, or boat, in which Noah and his family were allowed to escape the flood by which God destroyed the world, was afterwards venerated as a memorial of God's loving care for his chosen people – initially the Jews, subsequently all Christian believers (see Genesis chapters 6 to 9 for the story)
>
> **Which ... / ... despise** in all the surviving manuscripts of the poem, the last two lines of each **stanza** appear as one long line (containing seven stresses)
>
> **When I have put ... / ... and thee** these lines are in effect a prayer for death. John Donne is about to travel away from those he loves across the sea and into another country; he wishes also to travel away from his sins across the figurative sea of death into another life in heaven

in my winter that is, in the later stages of his life

controule cheek, limit. Neither Christ nor Christianity would put a check to the love in a soul in a condition of true spiritual harmony

Thou lov'st not ... thou free / My soule the demand is that God express his love for the poet by freeing his soul from the love of things or persons in this world, rather than God alone. In order to appreciate fully the severity of this prayer, it is necessary to remember that at this time John Donne had seven children to care for

Who ever gives, takes libertie for the image here, compare 'Batter my heart', lines 9–14, and the notes to those lines

Fame, Wit, Hopes John Donne had pursued these 'false mistresses' right up until his ordination in 1615

To see God only, I goe out of sight in order to see God and God alone, it is necessary to go where the human power of sight fails: that is, it is necessary to die

And to scape ... / ... Everlasting night the close of the poem repeats the prayer for death, in preference to the troubles of this life. The word 'chuse' (i.e., choose) makes it difficult not to feel that John Donne here goes beyond accepting death, and comes close to praying for it; the poem stands on the very edge of despair

HYMNE TO GOD MY GOD, IN MY SICKNESSE

According to Izaac Walton, this poem was written eight days before Donne's death in 1631; another contemporary witness, however, dates it December 1623, when Donne was seriously ill. Like the other Hymnes, the poem is a preparation for death, which is welcomed rather than feared.

that Holy roome heaven

Quire choir

I tune the Instrument (a) he prepares himself for death (so he himself is the instrument); and (b) he practises his skill in making hymns to God (so his poetic faculty is the instrument)

Whilst my Physitians ... / ... I their Mapp his doctors study him attentively, as geographers study a map

my South-west discoverie the South is the region of heat, the West the region where the sun declines. John Donne interprets his death by fever as the discovery of a route to a new world, i.e., to heaven

Per fretum febris these Latin words may be translated either (a) by the heat of fever, or (b) by the narrow passage (straits) of a fever

streights straits

my West his death

though theire currants ... to none although there is no return from the journey John Donne is about to make

As West and East / ... the Resurrection on a flat map of the world, the extreme West and the extreme East will be the same (as becomes apparent if the map is pasted on a globe); John Donne's West (his death) will also be his East (his resurrection, or rebirth in heaven)

Is the Pacifique Sea ... / ... Is *Jerusalem*? John Donne is thinking of the speculations by medieval geographers as to the location of the Garden of Eden, man's lost Paradise

Anyan probably Annam, formerly called 'Anian' and placed on the west coast of America, which medieval geographers believed to be separated by only a narrow strait from Asia

All streights ... are wayes to them the argument is that the straits of '*Anyan*, and *Magellan*, and *Gibraltare*' are the ways to the East, the Pacific and Jerusalem; however we travel to our eventual home in Paradise, we need to pass through narrow and difficult routes

Japhet ... Cham, or Sem Japhet, Ham and Shem were the three sons of Noah among whom the world was supposedly divided after the flood

We thinke ... / ... in one place it was sometimes held that the Crucifixion took place in what had formerly been the Garden of Eden ('Paradise'). 'Adams tree' is the tree of the knowledge of good and evil, the fruit of which Adam and Eve were forbidden by God

both *Adams* Christ was seen as a second Adam, especially in the theology of St Paul

the first *Adams* sweat at the time of the Fall, Adam was told 'in the sweat of thy face shalt thou eat bread' (see Genesis 3:19). John Donne is sweating because of the fever

in his purple wrapp'd ... / ... his other Crowne the argument is that as John Donne undergoes sufferings like those inflicted on Christ at the Crucifixion, so too he may hope to share in the promise of eternal life which Christ won for man by his self-sacrifice. The soldiers who executed Christ clothed him in mockery in a scarlet or purple robe, and a crown of thorns (see Matthew 27:28–9); by 'purple', however, John Donne may also be referring to Christ's blood, shed on man's behalf

Therefore ... the Lord throws down God is destroying John Donne physically in order to raise him to eternal life in heaven

A HYMNE TO GOD THE FATHER

This is the calmest and most eloquent of the Hymnes. It is both a prayer for forgiveness of sin, and a prayer for the conviction that his sins have been forgiven. The theological dilemma Donne confronts here is that his fear that he might not be saved – that he will perish on the shore, on the very border between life and death – is itself sinful, because it implies a doubt in God, and so might itself stand in the way of his salvation; the fear of sin can easily turn into the sin of fear.

'A Hymne to God the Father' resembles the sonnet 'Batter my heart', discussed above, in its concern that even when saved, and thus in Christian terms re-born and transformed, Donne should still be able to know himself as 'Donne': hence the play on his name throughout the poem.

that sinne where I begunne / ... done before original sin, that is, the corruption into which all men are born as a result of the Fall of Adam and Eve

those sinnes doe them still those sins that he commits every day

thou hast not done there is a deliberate **pun** here; the line means both (a) God has more to do, because there are yet more sins to forgive, and (b) God still does not have John Donne

that sinne... / Others to sinne John Donne may not have had anything in particular in mind here; it has been suggested that he is thinking of his abandonment of the Roman Catholic faith, the argument being that John Donne, secretly, continued to believe that the Roman Church was the only true Church of God. This reading would also suggest that John Donne's entire career in the Church of England was, in effect, encouraging others to sin as he had done. Others have suggested that John Donne might have been thinking of his secular love poetry, some of it (such as the elegy 'On his Mistris going to Bed') written in praise of infidelity and sexual freedom

when I have spunne / My last thred when he comes to the end of his life

the shore the very border of salvation

thy sonne / Shall shine this is one of John Donne's favourite puns, on the sun whose warmth is seen as an emblem of God's love for mankind, and on Christ the Son of God who died for mankind

Thou hast done the pun here resolves the poem; when once God has dealt with the poet's sin of fear, there is no more for God to do, and he will have gained the poet completely

PART THREE

CRITICAL APPROACHES

THEMES

Most readers come to John Donne through reading the *Songs and Sonets*, and one question they have understandably asked is what the collection of poems as a whole is about. If they are love poems, do they contain what might be called a philosophy of love? On the face of it, it seems unlikely. The poems were written over a long period of time, perhaps as much as twenty years, and Donne's attitudes no doubt changed a good deal during this period. However, there are a number of points which can be made about the view of love which emerges from the *Songs and Sonets*, even if these do not, in fact, add up to a 'philosophy'.

One point to be made at the outset is that there are many different kinds of relationship described or implied in these poems. The assumption in such poems as 'Womans Constancy' or 'The Flea', for example, is that the only thing which matters is sexual satisfaction; in contrast to this are such poems as 'A Valediction: forbidding mourning', where the poet scorns 'Dull sublunary lovers love' whose love depends on physical pleasure, and celebrates a love so 'refin'd' that it transcends or goes beyond sexuality.

Both the scorn for 'sublunary lovers love', and the insistence that true love is attainable only by a select few, are repeated in other poems, for example in 'The Extasie' and in 'The Canonization'. In both of these poems Donne speaks of love as a 'mysterie'. This is to suggest that love is a sacred state, which so exalts the lovers that they can claim to be a 'world' to themselves, and immune to the pressures of time and change. This idea of the self-sufficiency of the lovers is part of the argument of both 'The Good-morrow' and 'The Sunne rising', for example, in which the lovers set out to defy time, just as in 'A Valediction: forbidding mourning' they defy distance.

In many of the *Songs and Sonets*, however, the claim for the lovers' supremacy over the temporal world is accompanied by an acute sense of their vulnerability in a world dominated by time. The bravado of 'The Sunne rising' cannot blind us to the fact that the sun will rise and set regardless of the lover's boasts, and in 'The Anniversarie' the lovers' conviction that 'Here upon earth, we'are Kings' cannot obscure the fact that, at the last, 'Two graves must hide thine and my corse'. There is, too, always the fear of betrayal ('*If* our two loves be one'), and it is hard not to feel that the cynicism of 'The Apparition' or 'Loves Alchymie' derives from the memory of some such breach of faith. In this poem at least Donne is himself part of that despised 'layetie' which fails to see the 'mysterie' of love: 'Oh, 'tis imposture all'. Love in the *Songs and Sonets* may be 'so much refin'd, / That our selves know not what it is', but it still has to subsist in the ordinary or 'sublunary' world.

In a few poems (notably 'Loves Growth', 'Aire and Angels', and 'The Extasie') Donne does address himself directly to a philosophical question: that of the relation of body and soul in love. The argument of all three poems is that love is not 'pure' but 'elemented': that is to say, the mind and body are, if not equal, at least equally necessary to a full human love. Thus in 'The Extasie' the body is not seen as 'drosse', or waste material to be discarded, but as 'allay' (i.e., alloy – an element of little account on its own, but one which increases the strength of the whole compound). Donne's conclusion is that the loving self is hindered, and 'a great Prince in prison lies', unless body and soul can work together in harmony.

'The Extasie', then, contradicts both 'The Flea' (which ignores the spiritual element in love) and 'The Undertaking' (which denies the physical element, the 'Hee and Shee'). The only way, therefore, to construct a coherent 'philosophy of love' from the *Songs and Sonets* is to emphasise some poems at the expense of others; since this would obviously be improper, it seems better not to look for a carefully composed 'philosophy' of love, but to accept that Donne expressed different attitudes in different poems according to the mood of the moment. At the same time, however, it may be said that so many of the *Songs and Sonets* assert the dignity of love, and its claim on the entire self – both body and soul – that it seems reasonable to think that it is in these poems that the reader comes closest to discovering John Donne's usual feelings about love.

Questions about the techniques of John Donne's poetry have typically revolved around a few key terms, three in particular: **metaphysical**, **wit**, and the **conceit**. These terms are important, and they are discussed separately below. It might be helpful first to consider some of the other issues which might come under the heading of technique.

Rhythm

There is a note on Donne's handling of rhythm in the section Reading Donne, where it was suggested that most of the apparent problems can be resolved by reading the poems aloud, while attending to the emotional mood and intellectual logic of the poem as it develops. This is not to say that there is no problem. Ben Jonson's, Donne's contemporary and himself a great poet as well as a leading playwright, remarked that Donne deserved hanging because he failed to 'keep accent' – or, in other words, allowed himself a degree of freedom which Jonson thought excessive. Donne's poetry (like most English poetry) is predominantly **iambic**: that is, it alternates unstressed and stressed syllables, sometimes crudely represented by the phrase 'ti-tum'. Another way to represent the iambic pattern might be to say that the syllables alternate in the form: 1,2//1,2//1,2//1,2//1,2//– representing a five **foot** line, where the second syllable receives roughly twice the stress given to the first. This is the form, for example, of the first line of 'Loves Growth': 'I scarce beleeve my love to be so pure'. This feels normal to the English reader, in part because it is the stress pattern (and in this case also line length) used in most of Shakespeare's plays, but, if it were extended unbroken over many lines, it would of course become tedious, so we would expect it to be modified. The most frequently used modification is to reverse the first foot, or unit, producing a line of the form: 2,1//1,2//1,2//1,2//1,2//. This has the happy effect of giving the line a vigorous start, and it is a variation Donne uses frequently, as do Shakespeare and Milton; so, for example, in the first line of 'Loves Alchymie', the first word receives a contemptuous extra weight: 'Some that have deeper digg'd loves Myne than I'.

It was not this kind of modification that worried Ben Jonson, or leaves the modern reader sometimes uncertain. Consider again the first line of 'Loves Alchymie'. The stresses fall naturally on 'Some', on the first syllable of 'deeper', on 'digg'd', on 'Myne', and on 'I' at the end of the line.

But the line pattern is clearly more complex than the notation 1,2// etc. allows. The word 'loves' needs some stress too. The line, in fact, might be more precisely annotated in the form: 4,1//1,2//1,3//2,3//1,2// – where in each case, after the reversal of the pattern in the first foot, the second syllable receives more stress (so the pattern is iambic), but a notionally unstressed word ('loves') receives as much weight as a notionally stressed one elsewhere in the same line. Most of the difficulties of Donne's use of rhythm can be explained by reference to the idea, broadly, that he sometimes allows more weight to the unstressed syllables than more regular poets have been willing to do. In practice, what this means for the reader is that the poems often seem to be caught midway between the regularity of a formal pattern, and the complete freedom of impassioned speech; and it is through the tension between these two, each pulling the reader towards a slightly different emphasis, that the poetry gains so much of its energy. For an example of how this might affect our understanding of a poem, you might refer at this point to the discussions of lines 6–7 of 'The Anniversarie' in Text 5 of Extended Commentaries.

LANGUAGE

Ben Jonson made a further remark about Donne which has often been quoted: that he was 'the first poet in the world in some things, but for not being understood [he] would perish.' Donne has suffered from the reputation of being a 'difficult' poet, and one aim of this Note is to help with some of the genuine difficulties. But despite initial impressions, Donne's language is not difficult. In the first stanza of 'The Anniversarie', for example, fifty-six of the seventy-three words are **monosyllables**, and of the remaining seventeen only 'destruction' and perhaps 'everlasting' are in themselves complicated. This is roughly the pattern throughout Donne's verse. The difficulty, then, for the most part lies not in the language itself, but in the connections between ideas: in the logic and argument of the poem, and the relation of these to its mood or emotional temper.

There are two other points one might make about the language. The first is in fact rather a point about reference than about **diction.** Donne's poetry draws on and refers to whatever comes to mind; and Donne's was a remarkably well-informed mind. Later in this Note (see

Literary and Intellectual Background), in the discussion of what has sometimes been called 'the Elizabethan world picture', the point is made that Donne and his contemporaries tended to see the whole universe as interconnected, and as centred on man. So, for example, since the universe itself was made of the four elements (fire, earth, air and water), it was argued that man himself must be made of four qualities corresponding to these (the four 'humours', which formed the basis for much Elizabethan medicine). This habit, of seeing interconnections, seems to have been deeply ingrained in Donne. To take one example. In the poem 'Hymne to God my God, in my sicknesse', the relation between the elements and the humours underpins Donne's thought that the doctors who examine him, laid out on his bed, resemble men studying a map. But if a flat map is pasted on to a globe (it had only recently been discovered that the world was round), what had been its most distant edges are now joined together, so that far East meets the farthest point West. In the same way, Donne suggests, birth and death are (for the devout Christian believer) one and the same. Illness, map-making, voyages of discovery, the location of Christian sites (such as the Garden of Eden), Christian theology, the relation between sweat and tears, the possible parallel between books and bodies – all these are launched into the poem, and all are connected. We expect a poem about illness to deal with medicine, or with physical symptoms; but Donne typically reaches far beyond his immediate subject. Precisely the same point might be made about the love poems. Our experience, as we read a Donne poem for the first time, is of words and ideas tumbling in on us from all directions. The difficulty lies not in the words, nor even, necessarily, in the ideas Donne refers to, though often these are unfamiliar to the modern reader, but in the way one idea is linked to another.

The other point about Donne's language is a simpler one, and has to do with his use of **rhyme**. About one third of Donne's rhyme words are verbs – and, as noted above, typically they are monosyllables. So, in 'The Anniversarie', we have the following as rhyme words, standing at the end of the line, in a stressed position: passe, was, saw, draw, bee, prove, remove, bee, doe, refraine, attaine. The effect of this is to increase the sense of energy in the poem. We have the sense in reading Donne that nothing stays still. But the issue of Donne's intellectual restlessness leads on to his use of the **conceit**.

THREE KEY TERMS: METAPHYSICAL, WIT AND CONCEIT

We owe the word '**metaphysical**' as a critical term initially to the poet John Dryden (1631–1700), who complained that Donne 'affects the metaphysics, not only in his satires, but in his amorous verses, where nature only should reign': in other words, Donne employs the language of philosophical debate ('metaphysics') in contexts where it seemed to Dryden affected and inappropriate. Samuel Johnson took up Dryden's word and extended the charge in his 'Life of Cowley' (1779), which remains to this day the only item of secondary reading which every student of Donne needs to consult.

Johnson classed together a number of writers, including Donne, as 'the metaphysical poets'. (Donne did not think of himself in these terms, nor did he write a 'manifesto of metaphysical verse'.) Their common failing, according to Johnson, was that they had forsaken the true business of the poet, which was to represent either human nature or the natural world in such a way as to call upon the deepest feelings of the reader, and had instead written only in order to show off their unusual learning and their intellectual ingenuity – that is, their **wit**. Johnson found his evidence in the delight taken by these writers in the discovery of improbable and even fantastic points of comparison between things at first sight utterly unlike each other; such comparisons, when elaborated and made part of the argument of the poem, are known as **conceits**. Johnson provides several examples from the *Songs and Sonets*: the comparison of the lover's tears to the world in 'A Valediction: of weeping' (lines 10–18), and – the most often discussed of all metaphysical conceits – Donne's comparison of the continuing relationship of two lovers, even when parted, to the interdependent movements of the legs of a pair of compasses, in the last three **stanzas** of 'A Valediction: forbidding mourning'. However, the conceit may also appear in simpler and briefer forms, as in 'The Extasie':

> Loves mysteries in soules doe grow,
> But yet the body is his booke.

Sometimes a whole poem may be seen as the working out in detail of one central conceit, as is the case with 'The Flea', where Donne argues from the fact that the flea has bitten them both to the conclusion that 'wee almost, nay more than maryed are', or with 'Loves Alchymie', where the main conceit is that the lover who seeks love's 'hidden mysterie' is as deluded as the alchemist who seeks the elixir of life.

Johnson's apparent belief that where such passages of wit occur they must necessarily detract from the seriousness and emotional power of the poems has been challenged in the present century, in particular by T.S. Eliot in essays on 'The Metaphysical Poets' and on 'Andrew Marvell' (both first published in 1921, and reprinted in *Selected Essays*, Faber, London, 1932; enlarged edition 1951). Most critics have, however, been prepared to follow Johnson in regarding the use of such conceits as the defining characteristic of metaphysical poetry.

Other characteristic features of metaphysical poetry, including that of Donne, are closely related to the use of the conceit. Because the validity of the comparison is not immediately obvious, it has to be proved. Consequently, many of Donne's poems have an argumentative structure. A good example is 'Loves Growth', where the argument that love is 'elemented' rather than 'pure' is developed through a series of seemingly logical stages, marked by such terms and phrases as 'But if ...', 'And yet ...', 'If ...', 'For ...', 'As ...'. This quasi-logical structure helps to explain why the poems are often compressed and difficult: each line is intended to help the argument of the poem, and the reader is not allowed to relax.

This also explains why there is very little writing which is purely ornamental or descriptive in metaphysical poetry, and why the **diction** of metaphysical poetry is usually intellectual rather than sensuous. This is especially true of Donne, who favours words that are moral or evaluative rather than descriptive or evocative (that is, 'true', 'false', 'good', 'bad', rather than 'soft' or 'sweet'). Both these points may be illustrated from 'The Good-morrow', where we are not told what colour the lady's eyes are, or how lovely she is, but are instead asked to think about 'True plaine hearts' and about the possibility of permanency in love in a world of change.

As this last point suggests, the distinction between 'themes' and 'techniques' is not clear-cut. This is true of another characteristic of metaphysical verse, including Donne's, namely, its dramatic quality. Donne's poetry is dramatic in two senses. Firstly, most of the poems, both secular and divine, seem to arise out of particular situations – a man and a woman waking up in bed together, or celebrating an anniversary, or compelled to part, or a man confronting his God as he faces serious illness or the thought of damnation. Secondly, the language and movement of the verse are dramatic in that they are vivid, **colloquial**, and often suggestive of the rhythms of ordinary speech. The obvious examples are the opening lines of various poems ('For Godsake hold your tongue, and let me love', 'Batter my heart, three-person'd God'), but the point holds good for almost all of Donne's poetry.

This returns us to the terms 'metaphysical', 'wit', and 'conceit'. To stress the dramatic element in John Donne, as most modern readers do, is to emphasise the human interest of the verse. Yet this quality is exactly what Samuel Johnson felt was obscured by the use of the conceit; Johnson could not believe in the grief of a poet who compared his tears to coins, or parted lovers to a pair of compasses. Metaphysical poetry, including Donne's, constantly raises the question of the relation of the witty conceit to the emotional interest of a poem, but this is a general question to which there can be no general answer. In effect, Johnson is sometimes wrong, sometimes right. In describing Donne as a 'metaphysical poet', then, it should not be forgotten that metaphysical poetry is not all the same, and in the last analysis the differences between poems may matter far more than the features they have in common. 'Loves Growth' is not more typical of metaphysical poetry than, for example, 'The Will', but it is surely a far greater poem.

PART FOUR

EXTENDED COMMENTARIES

TEXT 1

The Sunne rising

> Busie old foole, unruly Sunne,
>> Why dost thou thus,
> Through windowes, and through curtains call on us?
> Must to thy motions lovers seasons run?
>> Sawcy pedantique wretch, goe chide
>> Late schoole boyes and sowre prentices,
>> Goe tell Court-huntsmen, that the King will ride,
>> Call countrey ants to harvest offices;
> Love, all alike, no season knowes, nor clyme,
> Nor houres, dayes, months, which are the rags of time.

>> Thy beames, so reverend, and strong
>> Why shouldst thou thinke?
> I could eclipse and cloud them with a winke,
> But that I would not lose her sight so long:
>> If her eyes have not blinded thine,
>> Looke, and to morrow late, tell mee,
>> Whether both the'India's of spice and Myne
>> Be where thou leftst them, or lie here with mee.
> Aske for those Kings whom thou saw'st yesterday,
> And thou shalt heare, All here in one bed lay.

>> She'is all States, and all Princes, I,
>> Nothing else is.
> Princes doe but play us; compar'd to this,
> All honor's mimique; All wealth alchimie.
>> Thou sunne art halfe as happy'as wee,
>> In that the world's contracted thus;
>> Thine age askes ease, and since thy duties bee
>> To warme the world, that's done in warming us.
> Shine here to us, and thou art every where;
> This bed thy center is, these walls, thy spheare.

The reference to the King in the first **stanza** dates this poem after 1603, and, therefore, after John Donne's marriage to Ann More in 1601; furthermore, the poem celebrates a completely satisfying union between two lovers who appear to dismiss the claims of the outside world, and this is a theme which may well have attracted Donne at a time when he had forfeited his post as Secretary to the Lord Keeper, and was virtually an exile from the world of affairs. For many readers, unduly influenced by the romantic story of a secret marriage, the poem is simply this: a glorious surrender to the joys of sexual love as the only true reality, and a splendid denial of the significance of the outside world. But to read 'The Sunne rising' in this way is to miss much of its richness and subtlety.

It is true that 'The Sunne rising' concentrates on the lovers at the warm centre, but Donne's lovers are at the centre of a living and attractive world. Donne gives full weight to their sense that they are, uniquely, immune from time:

> Love, all alike, no season knowes, nor clyme,
>
> Nor houres, dayes, months, which are the rags of time

and to their sense that they can afford to ignore the various claims of the world outside their bedroom:

> She'is all States, and all Princes, I,
>
> Nothing else is.

But he also admits into the poem the commonsense recognition that we all live, and love, in a world governed by time. The question in the fourth line, 'Must to thy motions lovers seasons run?', is phrased as if to invite the answer 'No', and the confidence with which the poem begins almost persuades us to give that answer. But the real answer is, of course, 'Yes', and the very presence of such a question reminds us that even the happiest lovers cannot escape being vulnerable to time and change, however arrogant or splendid their assertions to the contrary. Paradoxically, the recklessness with which Donne celebrates the idea that love is the only reality is made to carry with it an implicit confession of the absurdity of such a claim.

To describe 'The Sunne rising' as a paradoxical poem is not to deny that its immediate appeal is extraordinary. It opens with an irresistible energy, in which we recognise not only the determination to win an argument (ostensibly, with the sun, but in reality of course with the reader), but also the triumphant mood of a successful lover:

> Busie old foole, unruly Sunne,
> Why dost thou thus,
> Through windowes, and through curtaines call on us?

This is a remarkable stanza, and we are bound to be impressed by the worldly assurance of this lover who professes to care nothing for the world. Despite his complaint that the sun has disturbed them, there is nothing sleepy about his opening outburst; he is in fact already a great deal more alert and wide-awake, indeed more 'busie', than any of those who are reluctantly setting about their day's work. He is evidently not tempted to retreat from the world; he is, for example, far too sure of himself to regard the sun as a possible threat to his happiness, treating it instead as an incompetent but harmless servant to be sent about his business ('goe chide', 'goe tell'). In the same brisk manner the poet scoffs at 'the rags of time' as hardly meriting the lovers' attention, since love is of its very nature 'all alike' and, therefore, exempt from the pressures of time and change. But, we notice, the poet knows precisely what time it is out there in the world he contemplates with such lordly satisfaction: it's time for schoolboys and apprentices to hurry, for courtiers to escort the King out hunting, and for farmers to begin gathering the day's harvest. In short, although the first stanza of 'The Sunne rising' overtly denies the significance of anything outside the lovers' bedroom, it is hard to imagine ten lines which could set the lovers down more firmly in the midst of the day-to-day realities of the ordinary, familiar world.

It is, moreover, the poet's intense delight in the particular 'rag of time' the poem celebrates, a little after sunrise, that inspires the outrageous challenge to the sun's supremacy in the second stanza:

> Thy beames, so reverend, and strong
> Why shouldst thou thinke?
> I could eclipse and cloud them with a winke,

The reader may feel tempted here to intervene on behalf of the sun, by pointing out the absurd conceit of this: the poet's defiant gesture would, after all, merely leave him in the dark and the sun shining as warmly as ever. But Donne knows this perfectly well, and has his answer ready almost before we can put forward the objection:

> I could eclipse and cloud them with a winke,
> But that I would not lose her sight so long:

It is a marvellous moment in the poem; we can hardly continue to accuse the poet of sentimental self-deception when he has so neatly outwitted us with this unexpected reply. Donne deftly concedes that 'her sight' is revealed to him by a sun which shines with just the same brilliance for kings and schoolboys as for the lovers, and at the same time he refuses to withdraw the claim that only their love is real. The effect here is a little like that of the double-edged question in line four of the first stanza: Donne gives us the lovers' denial of the ordinary world, acknowledges the ultimate impossibility of such defiance, and continues, undisturbed, to insist on the unique reality of the lovers' experience.

Donne's manner becomes still more exuberant as he seeks to pay tribute to all that is precious about 'her sight':

> If her eyes have not blinded thine,
> Looke, and to morrow late, tell mee,

– 'late' offers a sly reminder that the sun should not repeat its mistake of intruding upon them too early –

> Whether both the'India's of spice and Myne
> Be where thou leftst them, or lie here with mee.
> Aske for those Kings whom thou saw'st yesterday,
> And thou shalt heare, All here in one bed lay.

The extravagance of this is felt as a compliment to the woman. It is a way of registering his sense of immeasurable contentment in her presence, a presence so richly delighting that it has converted their bedroom into a treasure-house of wealth and perfume (she is 'both the'India's of spice and Myne' – not just one or the other). It would be untrue to his sense of her for Donne to speak more modestly; he needs to reach out for the most extravagant terms available to him, and the boldness with which he does so corresponds to the generosity of her gift of herself.

But there is an element of folly in all boasting, and it does not necessarily cease to appear ridiculous because it is done in **verse**, and by a lover. In the third stanza Donne faces this difficulty, and characteristically turns it to his advantage by carrying his extravagance to the point where it collapses:

> She'is all States, and all Princes, I,
> Nothing else is.

The two previous stanzas have been leading towards just such an effect (the question in line 4, the challenge in lines 11–14), but even so the reader is left wondering at the audacity of this; the pause which follows the short second line is filled up with our astonishment. Donne's boastful, loving claim is made with a recklessness that draws attention to itself, and in doing so effectively concedes the absurdity of the boast; there is, after all, a world outside the bedroom window, and its existence has been acknowledged from the first stanza onwards. Donne hints briefly that he has arguments in readiness which would prove that this world is merely an illusion:

> Princes doe but play us; compar'd to this,
> All honor's mimique; All wealth alchimie.

But the whole poem has shown him to be so entirely at home in the world that such arguments would clearly be out of place here, and they are taken no further. Instead, Donne relaxes into a mood of humorous condescension, as the sun which had been driven from the room in the first stanza is re-admitted with a forgiving reference to its great age:

> Thou sunne art half as happy'as wee,
> In that the world's contracted thus;
> Thine age asks ease, and since thy duties bee
> To warme the world, that's done in warming us.

In the closing lines, Donne re-affirms the impossible claim of the poem, not now in the manner of one consciously defending a paradox – he has already gone as far as it is possible to go in that direction – but with a **rhythm** suggesting complete assurance:

> Shine here to us, and thou art every where;
> This bed thy center is, these walls, thy spheare.

The argumentative bustle with which the poem began, as Donne turned away from the woman to quarrel with the sun, finds its perfect answer in the poised quietness of this conclusion, as he returns to her and to the warmth of their love-making.

'The Sunne rising', then, is more than the simple poem it is often taken to be by those who would see it as Donne's ecstatic response to his life with Ann More. Donne celebrates the supreme reality of love, but he refuses to dismiss the world as merely darkness; the paradox of the poem lies in John Donne's insistence that the two conflicting claims, of love and of the world, must both be met in full.

TEXT 2

The Apparition

When by thy scorne, O murdresse, I am dead,
          And that thou thinkst thee free
From all solicitation from mee,
Then shall my ghost come to thy bed,
And thee, fain'd vestall, in worse armes shall see;
Then thy sicke taper will begin to winke,
And he, whose thou art then, being tyr'd before,
Will, if thou stirre, or pinch to wake him, thinke
          Thou call'st for more,
And in false sleepe will from thee shrinke,
And then poore Aspen wretch, neglected thou
Bath'd in a cold quicksilver sweat wilt lye
          A veryer ghost then I;
What I will say, I will not tell thee now,
Lest that preserve thee'; and since my love is spent,
I'had rather thou shouldst painfully repent,
Then by my threatnings rest still innocent.

'The Sunne rising', highly individual as it is, belongs to a recognised poetic tradition, that of the **aubade** or 'dawn-song'. In 'The Apparition', a quite different but equally characteristic poem, Donne demonstrates his individuality by interweaving two themes familiar to any reader of sixteenth-century poetry: the rejected lover's complaint that his lady's chastity is killing him, and the warning that the lady will one day long in vain for the pleasures she now refuses to grant her lover. The effect of combining the two themes is to transform them both:

> When by thy scorne, O murdresse, I am dead,
>> And that thou thinkst thee free
> From all solicitation from mee,
> Then shall my ghost come to thy bed,
> And thee, fain'd vestall, in worse armes shall see;
> Then thy sicke taper will begin to winke

The first line here apparently acknowledges the conventions of **Petrarchan** poetry in supposing that the rejected lover will die of unrequited love, but in every other respect this is an anti-Petrarchan poem. The lover's bitterness towards his lady is seemingly at least a match for her scorn towards him, and rather than passively lament the cruelty which is supposedly killing him, he takes a malicious pleasure in contemplating the suffering he, in his turn, will cause her. The routine poetic idea of dying for love is being used to set in motion a far from routine poem.

If the speaker is unwilling to play the part assigned by convention to the Petrarchan lover, no more is the lady quite what the Petrarchan conventions required her to be, and it soon appears that there are more straightforward charges to be brought against her than the merely customary one that she has been unkind:

> And he, whose thou art then, being tyr'd before,
> Will, if thou stirre, or pinch to wake him, thinke
>> Thou call'st for more,
> And in false sleepe will from thee shrinke,

The 'fain'd vestall' has claimed to prize her virginity, above all else in order to justify refusing herself to the would-be lover, but at her bedside his ghost will see the humiliating truth: that her sexual appetite is in fact far keener than that of the lover she has that night exhausted, and who 'shrinks' away from her in fear of further demands on his tired manhood. The lines are brutal, both in the matter-of-fact treatment of her sexual desires ('pinch', 'thinke / Thou call'st for more'), and in the suggestion that she has been casual and indiscriminate in acquiring her lovers ('in worse armes', 'he, whose thou art then'). The lines which follow allow her no respite:

> And then poore Aspen wretch, neglected thou
> Bath'd in a cold quicksilver sweat wilt lye
> A veryer ghost then I;

This is to portray human sexuality at its most mundane, least glamorous level. It would be hard to imagine anything more remote from the elevated tone of the Petrarchan poets than this contemptuous picture of the lady sweating and trembling beside her unresponsive lover.

The poem appears to have reached its climax with these lines: the speaker has his revenge upon the lady – ignored by the lover she has accepted, and tormented by the lover she had spurned, she is still more dead-alive than he is ('A veryer ghost than I') – and at the same time he has managed to startle and amuse his readers by so thoroughly subverting the conventions of Petrarchism. But it is a part of Donne's genius that he seems always to have more to offer than the reader has anticipated. Here the unlooked-for twist comes in the last four lines:

> What I will say, I will not tell thee now,
> Lest that preserve thee'; and since my love is spent,
> I'had rather thou shouldst painfully repent,
> Then by my threatnings rest still innocent.

He declares that his love is finished ('spent'), but of course the whole basis of the poem is his continuing but hopeless desire for her. If we have been tempted to approach the poem biographically, reading it (as some have done) as if it were Donne's heartfelt outcry against a woman who had in real life refused his advances, we shall have to consider these closing lines as a blemish, a passage of futile bravado. But Donne deliberately leaves us with a mocking picture of the lover as a man who has failed during his lifetime to find words with which to woo the lady, and who is therefore reduced to threatening her with the terrible things he is sure he will be able to think of once he has died for love. These last four lines should be seen not as a slip, but as the final witty stroke in a carefully, controlled poem which, without them, might appear too one-sided and savage to be entertaining. 'The

Apparition' serves as a further reminder that we should not uncritically identify the historical Donne with the person who is made to speak in the poems.

TEXT 3

The Good-morrow

I wonder by my troth, what thou, and I
Did, till we lov'd? were we not wean'd till then?
But suck'd on countrey pleasures, childishly?
Or snorted we in the seaven sleepers den?
T'was so; But this, all pleasures fancies bee.
If ever any beauty I did see,
Which I desir'd, and got, t'was but a dreame of thee.

And now good morrow to our waking soules,
Which watch not one another out of feare;
For love, all love of other sights controules,
And makes one little roome, an every where.
Let sea-discoverers to new worlds have gone,
Let Maps to other, worlds on worlds have showne,
Let us possesse our world, each hath one, and is one.

My face in thine eye, thine in mine appeares,
And true plaine hearts doe in the faces rest,
Where can we finde two better hemispheares
Without sharpe North, without declining West?
What ever dyes, was not mixt equally;
If our two loves be one, or, thou and I
Love so alike, that none doe slacken, none can die.

The central **image** in 'The Good-morrow' and the one that gives the poem its title, is that of the two lovers waking up into a new world of love. It is a brave image, and there is much that is brave and exciting about the poem: notably, the courage with which Donne seeks to acknowledge the past and the future as well as the present reality of their love, and the ambition which leads him to include so wide a range of feeling and mood in the short space of twenty-one lines. How far the courage and the ambition are eventually justified by the success of the poem as a poem, that is, as something which is a shaped work of art as well as a moving document of human experience, is, however, an open question.

The first few lines of 'The Good-morrow' are often cited, quite justly, to illustrate the remarkable directness of Donne's poetic voice, so closely related to the realistic expressiveness being developed by the dramatists throughout the 1590s:

> I wonder by my troth, what thou, and I
> Did, till we lov'd? were we not wean'd till then?
> But suck'd on countrey pleasures, childishly?
> Or snorted we in the seaven sleepers den?
> T'was so;

John Donne has two related tasks here: firstly, to recognise the fact that both he and she have loved before ('what *thou*, and *I* / Did' – emphasis added), and secondly, to insist that what they are now discovering together is at last the real world of love, and not merely another realm of 'fancies'. It would be dishonest to ignore the past; indecent to dwell on it unduly. Donne accepts it, as he must, but without alarm, and deprives it of any power to harm them by converting it into a series of comic affairs marked by hopeful enthusiasm and graceless incompetence in about equal measure. The vocabulary is at once affectionate and dismissive: 'not wean'd', 'suck'd', 'childishly', 'snorted'. The bungled 'countrey pleasures' of the past, which might have become a barrier between them, provide instead an opportunity for them to express their love in shared laughter.

But it is not easy to make the transition from laughter to affirmation. Donne is attempting, after all, to say what not only every lover but also every libertine would say: that his other women meant nothing to him in comparison with his love for her. The problem is to make the claim carry conviction:

> T'was so; But this, all pleasures fancies bee.
> If ever any beauty I did see,
> Which I desir'd, and got, t'was but a dreame of thee.

We can probably pass over the rather disparaging 'any beauty', but it is more difficult to know how to respond to 'and got', an unnecessary and almost brutal aside, which seems rather to flaunt his past loves than simply to acknowledge them. What purports to be sexual honesty looks disagreeably like sexual showing-off: 'Whenever I wanted a beautiful woman, I always had her.' Such showing-off is not readily compatible with honesty, and coming where it does the smoothly reassuring 't'was but a dreame of thee' is perhaps too smooth to be very convincing. There is a hint of aggression here, which clashes uncomfortably with the shared amusement of the opening lines.

In the second **stanza** Donne turns from the past to the present. It was 'feare', we now understand, which marred the earlier effort at candour, and gave rise to the harshness of tone at the close of the first stanza. In this poem, as in a number of others ('The Anniversarie', 'A Valediction: forbidding mourning', 'A Lecture upon the Shadow'), Donne shows himself acutely aware of the possibility that love will be invaded by fear. At the same time, he seems instinctively to recognise that while we cannot banish fear, we can nonetheless rise free of it. The effect of this recognition, wherever it comes, is profoundly moving. Here, the lovely movement of the verse signals the lovers' sudden emergence from a state of suspicious watchfulness into a world of mutual contemplation, both delighted and delighting:

> And now good morrow to our waking soules,
> Which watch not one another out of feare;
> For love, all love of other sights controules,
> And makes one little roome, an every where.

By the most natural and unobtrusive of images, their literal awakening after (we assume) a night of love-making is made to suggest the awakening of their souls into a new clarity of feeling, a new certainty. It comes to them almost as a gift, to which they can respond only with wonderment, expressed in the simplest of greetings: 'And now good morrow to our waking soules'. The 'love of other sights', which might have been so damaging, has been brought calmly under control by the power of 'love' itself; so that what the lovers experience is not self-denial, or a willed limitation of self, but release, and the liberating discovery of the other:

> Let sea-discoverers to new worlds have gone,
>
> Let Maps to other, worlds on worlds have showne,
>
> Let us possesse our world, each hath one, and is one.

There is a wealth of meaning here in the word 'possesse'. It carries the suggestion both of 'self-possession', the state of mind most unlike 'feare', and of 'sexual possession', which is so much more than the mere squandering of sexual energies the lovers had known previously ('I wonder ... what thou, and I / *Did*' – emphasis added) There is, too, the further suggestion that the lovers have progressed from a lower to a higher level of existence. They 'possesse' their world, an 'every where' found without struggle in 'one little roome', and in doing so they have reached a goal denied to the explorers and astronomers who voyage across the seas or scan the heavens in search of remote 'new worlds' they can conquer or study, but never in any full sense 'possesse'. The explorers and astronomers, we may say, remain trapped in the realm of Action, while the lovers have, as if by a miracle, moved beyond them into the realm of Being.

Such terms seem especially appropriate at the beginning of the third stanza, where the mood of the lovers is one of trance-like stillness:

> My face in thine eye, thine in mine appeares,
>
> And true plaine hearts doe in the faces rest,

– the deep mutual gaze, in which they each find themselves in the eyes of the other, and then the growing certainty that here at last is the complete candour which could not quite be achieved earlier in the poem. The lovers, their fears and their false starts now behind them, appear to have arrived at a point of 'rest' where all further struggle is unnecessary. But, movingly, the poem is not allowed to 'rest' here. The promise of an ideal stability leads Donne to think about the future, and immediately the note of doubt and uncertainty begins to re-appear:

> Where can we finde two better hemispheares
>
> Without sharpe North, without declining West?

The argument that their world of love will be exempt from any coldness of feeling ('sharpe North') or any falling-off of attachment ('declining West') is made to depend upon the obvious logical absurdity of a sphere consisting solely of the South and the East; the effect of the **image** is to suggest that permanency in love is not a real possibility, as if the world they have discovered together ('our world') were, after all, only an illusion. Donne tries an alternative argument, borrowing this time from medieval doctrines, both scientific and religious, as to the causes of disease and decay:

> What ever dyes, was not mixt equally;
> If our two loves be one, or, thou and I
> Love so alike, that none doe slacken, none can die.

The theory behind these lines is that whatever dies or decays does so because of a lack of unity or balance in the elements of which it was composed. If, therefore, the lovers really do make up one world, or if at least their two loves are so exactly matched that there can be no decay, then there can be no death of love for them. The logic of this is, however, decidedly strained, and the possibility of a **punning** reference to the male orgasm ('slacken', 'die') only complicates the lines still further. It is a strange way to conclude a poem with so optimistic a title.

Two lines from another of Donne's poems, 'A Lecture upon the Shadow', help to explain what is happening in this final stanza:

> Love is a growing, or full constant light;
> And his first minute, after noone, is night.

The power of love to irradiate the whole experience of the lovers provides the occasion for some of the most memorable of the *Songs and Sonets*. But if it is true that few English poets have so movingly celebrated the joys of a fulfilled love, it is also true that few others – perhaps only Shakespeare and Thomas Hardy (1840–1928) – have been so conscious of how easily a single 'minute' of doubt can darken all the mid-day brightness of love, transforming joy into despair, and mutual confidence into suspicion. The vulnerability of human love in a world dominated by time and change is a recurrent theme in the *Songs and Sonets,* and the essential subject of 'The Good-morrow'. None of the moods expressed in this poem is entirely stable, not even the quiet serenity of the central section. There is a brave attempt in the first stanza to dispel the fears arising from the recognition that the lovers have not always possessed their world of love, but it is only partly successful, and the poem concludes with their newly discovered clarity of feeling under threat from the fear that this world may one day be lost to them. They have not always loved each other; there may come a time when they no longer do so: this is the thought that hovers behind the last five lines of the poem. The whole conclusion is shot through with uncertainty. This is most obvious in the last two lines, where Donne is apparently unable to decide whether their 'two loves' are 'one', or merely 'alike', but there is uncertainty too in the melancholy echoing of 'none … none', and in the **rhythm** of the final line, which carries the poem haltingly to a stop on the word 'die'. Donne puts forward arguments to prove that their world of love is secure, but his arguments serve only to reveal that there can be no such proofs of security, and the poem closes on a note far removed from the vigorous confidence of the opening lines.

Not all readers of John Donne will accept this account of the poem, and even among those who do accept it, there may be disagreement as to how far the poem is successful. It may be objected that Donne attempts too much in a poem of only three stanzas, and that too much is made to depend on the reader's ability to recognise and interpret the constant shifts of mood and tone. These two charges may be resolved into the larger and more general one, that the poem is just too complicated to be read with pleasure.

There is no simple answer to these objections, which were already to be heard during Donne's lifetime; a whole history of taste could be written around the question of what degree of difficulty is allowable in poetry. It is, however, broadly true that most readers of poetry in the sixteenth century expected the kinds of pleasure to be found, albeit in rather a limited way, in such a poem as the anonymous 'Smooth are thy looks' (quoted on pages 119–20 of this Note): the kinds of pleasure afforded, for example, by clarity of tone and by obvious symmetries of form. Then, at the end of the century, Donne and some of his contemporaries, including Shakespeare, began to offer satisfactions of a new and different kind, by writing **verse** whose most notable characteristic is its imaginative truthfulness to the nature of human experience. Where that is complex, as it is in 'The Good-morrow', the verse is correspondingly tortuous and difficult. The human experience of love is that the line which separates security from fear is extremely fragile; Donne sacrifices the formal pleasures of clarity and symmetry and the like, in order to write of the crossing and re-crossing of that line. The result is a poem of continually shifting moods, which even an experienced reader may find difficult to interpret with confidence.

In the last analysis, the question is one of different kinds of poetic pleasure. Fortunately we are not obliged to grade them, or to choose between them. Twentieth-century readers have, by and large, grown accustomed to wrestling with poetry of considerable difficulty, and this has certainly done much to ease the advance of Donne's reputation. This is all to the good, but the tendency to undervalue other and simpler forms of poetry should be resisted. The poet and critic T.S. Eliot (1888–1965), discussing the difficulty of modern poetry, suggested that 'for some periods of society a more relaxed form of writing is right, and for others a more concentrated' (in *The Use of Poetry and the Use of Criticism*, Faber, London, 1933.) We can sensibly reapply Eliot's words, and say that what is true for some periods will equally be true for some readers. There is room in poetry for 'Smooth are thy looks' as well as for 'The Goodmorrow'.

TEXT 4

Loves Alchymie, or Mummy

Some that have deeper digg'd loves Myne then I,
Say, where his centrique happinesse doth lie:
        I have lov'd, and got, and told,
But should I love, get, tell, till I were old,
I should not finde that hidden mysterie;
        Oh, 'tis imposture all:
And as no chymique yet th'Elixar got,
        But glorifies his pregnant pot,
        If by the way to him befall
Some odoriferous thing, or medicinall,
        So, lovers dreame a rich and long delight,
        But get a winter-seeming summers night.

Our ease, our thrift, our honor, and our day,
Shall we, for this vaine Bubles shadow pay?
        Ends love in this, that my man,

> Can be as happy'as I can; If he can
> Endure the short scorne of a Bridegroomes play?
>   That loving wretch that sweares,
>   'Tis not the bodies marry, but the mindes,
>   Which he in her Angelique findes,
>   Would sweare as justly, that he heares,
> In that dayes rude hoarse minstralsey, the spheares.
>   Hope not for minde in women; at their best,
>   Sweetnesse, and wit, they'are but *Mummy*, possest.

It is a startling but instructive experience to turn from 'The Good-morrow' to 'Loves Alchymie'. 'The Good-morrow' is a poem of great complexity, marked by uncertainty and by abrupt and puzzling shifts of tone, whose most moving effect is, even so, to evoke fulfilled love as a condition of absolute peace. 'Loves Alchymie' is, in contrast, the most direct of all the *Songs and Sonets*, and utterly insistent on the impossibility of such a condition: 'Oh, 'tis imposture all'. Disillusion, anger and pain are all present in the poem, but fused together rather than treated as so many separate moods, so that the tone of the poem is one of unbroken harshness. The result is a poem of undeniable power; the critical question is to know how to respond to such a display of power.

The **imagery** which opens the poem is both ugly and violent, as if Donne were mounting an assault upon the reader:

> Some that have deeper digg'd loves Myne then I,
> Say, where his centrique happinesse doth lie:
>   I have lov'd, and got, and told,
> But should I love, get, tell, till I were old,
> I should not finde that hidden mysterie;
>   Oh, 'tis imposture all:

To write of sexual love in this way is to eliminate any sense of tenderness, or indeed of any human feeling other than brutal rapacity. The woman is simply a mine to be ransacked, and the **rhythm** and **alliteration** suggest a kind of sexual stabbing ('Some that have deeper digg'd loves Myne than I'). The poet has 'lov'd, and got, and told', but the word 'lov'd', as it is used here, has become as empty of meaning for him as were the various women whose bodies have been plundered in the pursuit of love's 'centrique happinesse'. Successive disappointments in the search have led him only to the conviction that those who told him of the mysteries, or sacred truths of love, were liars and impostors; there is no 'hidden mysterie'. Or, if they were not deliberate cheats, then they were fools deceived by their own longings:

> And as no chymique yet th'Elixar got,
>> But glorifies his pregnant pot,
>> If by the way to him befall
> Some odoriferous thing, or medicinall,

There is an extraordinary weight of contempt in these lines. Donne almost certainly has in mind the conventional literary portrayal of the alchemist as a man whose life was spent among foul smells in dark and dirty rooms; the suggestion is, then, that lover and alchemist resemble each other not only in being deluded, but also in needing the encouragement offered by the occasional discovery of some sweeter smell than usual – 'Some odoriferous thing'.

The last two lines of the **stanza** have the force of an **epigram**:

> So, lovers dreame a rich and long delight,
> But get a winter-seeming summers night.

The rhyme-words ('delight' / 'night') provide a succinct summary of the main theme of the poem: the gulf between the warmth and happiness of which the lover dreams, and the harshness of the reality which eventually confronts him – as soon over as a summer's night, but as cold and bleak as a night in winter.

The second stanza is as embittered as the first, with the stress failing on a sense of personal despoilment. It opens with two questions, the first of which strikingly recalls the experience dramatised in Shakespeare's famous Sonnet 129, 'The expense of spirit in a waste of shame' (with which Donne's poem may usefully be compared; both poems are expressions of extreme sexual nausea, in language of extreme brutality):

> Our ease, our thrift, our honor, and our day,
> Shall we, for this vaine Bubles shadow pay?

The term 'thrift' denotes the careful management of resources, usually financial. Here, however, it is the resources of the inner self which have been wasted; peace of mind ('Our ease'), personal honour, even physical health ('our day'), have all been thrown away in a vain attempt to win a happiness which has, so the poet declares, no more substance than the shadow of a bubble.

The insistent theme of the poem is hammered out again in the following lines:

> Ends love in this, that my man,
> Can be as happy'as I can; If he can
> Endure the short scorne of a Bridegroomes play?
> That loving wretch that sweares,
> 'Tis not the bodies marry, but the mindes,
> Which he in her Angelique findes,
> Would sweare as justly, that he heares,
> In that dayes rude hoarse minstralsey, the spheares.

There is no mystery of love, and no music of the spheres to be heard by those alone whose souls have awakened; love exists only at a level so commonplace that even to think of it fills the poet with disgust ('the short scorne of a Bridegroomes play', 'that dayes rude hoarse minstralsey'). This disgust rises to a sickening climax in the final **couplet**:

> Hope not for minde in women; at their best
> Sweetnesse and wit, they'are but *Mummy*, possest.

'Mummy' was the term used for pieces of flesh which had been artificially preserved for the sake of their supposed medicinal value. To possess a woman sexually, then, is to enter a mindless lump of dead flesh: a revolting experience, but one which may offer temporary relief from the loss of 'ease'. The other relevant sense of 'possest' adds the equally brutal suggestion that the appearance of life in the woman – even her apparent 'Sweetnesse and wit' – comes only from the fact that the dead flesh has been possessed, or taken over, by an evil spirit or demon. The encounter with such a spirit is, according to the poet, the reality which awaits those who have pursued the dream of love as a marriage of true minds.

'Loves Alchymie' is obviously not a pleasant poem, but it is, once read, not soon forgotten, and it is difficult to know what to make of it. The difficulty is not, this time, caused by problems of interpretation, since the poem could hardly be more straightforward; nor is it simply a matter of our being disturbed by the attitudes expressed in it. Rather, it has to do with our sense that here all the powers of a considerable intelligence have been marshalled to the sole end of forcing the reader's assent. The poet has already confessed himself relentless in seeking love's 'centrique happinesse' – he has, to use his own brutal image, dug deep and often ('I have lov'd, and got, and told') – and he is no less relentless in pursuing his attack upon the illusion, as he now believes it to be, that there is some 'hidden mysterie' in love. He maintains one idea throughout the poem, in one tone of voice; no resistance is tolerated from the reader, just as none was tolerated from the women. Our difficulty with the poem is, in other words, that Donne is so obviously intent on bullying the reader into submission; 'Loves Alchymie' may be described as an example of the abuse of literary power.

There is another point which needs to be made about this poem. 'Loves Alchymie' is filled with disillusion; but where there is disillusion, there must formerly have been hope. The 'loving wretch' upon whom Donne pours such scorne in the second stanza is in fact none other than Donne himself, in such poems as 'The Extasie', where he speaks of 'Loves mysteries' (line 71), or 'A Valediction: forbidding mourning', where there is no doubting the conviction, mocked in 'Loves Alchymie', that ''Tis not the bodies marry, but the mindes':

> But we by'a love, so much refin'd,
> > That our selves know not what it is,
> Inter-assured of the mind,
> > Care lesse, eyes, lips, and hands to misse.

Here, surely, one finds the 'hidden mysterie' of love which is so fiercely denied in 'Loves Alchymie'. The force of the word 'mysterie' is to suggest that the sacred truths of love, like those of religion, cannot be commanded by the will, or won by 'digging' and 'getting'. They can, however, be revealed; it is just such a revelation, or sudden gift of truth, which is celebrated in the second stanza of 'The Good-morrow'. But in that poem, as so often in the *Songs and Sonets*, Donne is also concerned with the terrifying vulnerability of such moments of vision:

> Love is a growing, or full constant light;
> And his first minute, after noone, is night. ('A Lecture upon the Shadow')

'Loves Alchymie' is a poem written out of the darkness of that night which, in the *Songs and Sonets*, is only one minute's journey from the fulfilled love of 'The Good-morrow'. Violently opposed though the two poems are, the idealism of the one and the cynicism of the other are nonetheless the twin poles of the human experience of love in a world subject to all the pressures of time and change.

TEXT 5

The Anniversarie

All Kings, and all their favorites,
    All glory of honors, beauties, wits,
The Sun it selfe, which makes times, as they passe,
Is elder by a yeare, now, then it was
When thou and I first one another saw:
All other things, to their destruction draw,
    Only our love hath no decay;
This, no to morrow hath, nor yesterday,
Running it never runs from us away,
But truly keepes his first, last, everlasting day.

    Two graves must hide thine and my coarse,
    If one might, death were no divorce,
Alas, as well as other Princes, wee,
(Who Prince enough in one another bee,)
Must leave at last in death, these eyes, and eares,
Oft fed with true oathes, and with sweet salt teares;
    But soules where nothing dwells but love
(All other thoughts being inmates) then shall prove
This, or a love increased there above,
When bodies to their graves, soules from their graves
    remove.

    And then wee shall be throughly blest,
    But wee no more, then all the rest;
Here upon earth, we'are Kings, and none but wee
Can be such Kings, nor of such subjects bee.

> Who is so safe as wee? where none can doe
> Treason to us, except one of us two.
>   True and false feares let us refraine,
> Let us love nobly, and live, and adde againe
> Yeares and yeares unto yeares, till we attaine
> To write threescore: this is the second of our raigne.

'The Anniversarie' is among the most eloquent of the *Songs and Sonets*. It is a meditation on the lovers' sense of the timelessness of their world of love, and on the relationship of this to the world of time in which all human love necessarily takes place, and which is of course logically implied by the fact that this is a poem about the anniversary of the lovers' first meeting. The claim is that their love is immune from the pressure of time:

> This, no to morrow hath, nor yesterday,
> Running it never runs from us away,
> But truly keepes his first, last, everlasting day.

Theirs is an 'everlasting day' of love which takes them beyond any concern with 'yesterday' or 'to morrow'. But it soon becomes clear that this claim is at odds with the impetus behind the poem, which is, firstly, to celebrate the fact that they have now enjoyed a whole year of yesterdays together, and secondly, to anticipate a series of equally happy tomorrows – a series which, Donne is later to admit, no amount of good faith or good fortune can possibly make 'everlasting' (albeit the lovers can hope that nothing less than the limits of life itself will bring their days together to an end). In short, to celebrate an 'Anniversarie' (literally a 'returning yearly') is also to concede that even lovers have to submit to the world of time.

There is, clearly, a strong thematic resemblance between 'The Anniversarie' and 'The Sunne rising':

> Love, all like, no season knowes, nor clyme,
> Nor houres, dayes, months, which are the rags of time.

But 'The Anniversarie' is an altogether quieter poem, the tone sober rather than delightedly paradoxical. The opening lines request our attention instead of demanding it:

> All Kings, and all their favorites,
> All glory of honors, beauties, wits,
> The Sun it selfe, which makes times, as they passe,
> Is elder by a yeare, now, then it was
> When thou and I first one another saw:

The poem begins as if John Donne is preparing to acclaim the mighty ones of the earth – the kings and their favourites, the honoured, the beautiful, the clever – but the verse sweeps on, and it becomes clear that they are mentioned in order that he may record that they, too, are moving on towards their graves. Even the sun, customarily the symbol of all that is glorious and powerful, is presented not as the monarch of the temporal world but as its chief victim, making times only to be itself made older by them, 'as they passe'. There is no place here for the mocking laughter directed against 'the rags of time' in 'The Sunne rising'. Instead, the transience of all things is acknowledged, with measured calmness, as one of the central facts of human existence.

But here, as always in the *Songs and Sonets*, the lovers must make a stand against the power of time:

> All other things, to their destruction draw,
> Only our love hath no decay;
> This, no to morrow hath, nor yesterday,
> Running it never runs from us away,
> But truly keepes his first, last, everlasting day.

The steady movement of the verse invites us to consider where the stresses should fall, and, no matter how we may eventually decide to hear the lines, to allow at least some weight to the alternatives. We need to be aware, in other words, both of the emphatic '*All* other things ... ' followed by the timid daring of '*Only* our love ...', and of the more dismissive 'All *other things* ...' followed by the bold pride of 'Only *our love* hath *no* decay'. The one reading seems to concede too much, and the other too little, to the universal drawing-on towards destruction; our sense that both readings are required is an indication of the difficulties Donne faces in dealing with the theme of an anniversary.

There is another way to describe these difficulties. The essential impulse behind the poem is one which is entirely familiar in life as in literature: the lover's wish to say 'I will love you for ever'. But it is obvious that an element of falseness generally attaches to such declarations; to the extent that we are all not only mortal but changeable – liable, in fact, to 'decay' as well as to 'destruction' – we need to be extremely wary about how we lay claim to 'for ever'. Once we have recognised this, we may feel obliged to judge all such avowals severely, as a species of dishonesty, or at the least to agree with Samuel Johnson in seeing them as evidence of human folly; vows, he wrote (in a note on Shakespeare's play, *Love's Labour's Lost*), 'proceed commonly from a presumptuous confidence, and a false estimate of human powers'. But there is surely something else that also needs to be recognised: that an increased confidence, and an enlarged estimate of human powers, are among the necessary conditions for love to exist at all; for without these, love would be cancelled almost before it began by the fear and watchfulness of which Donne writes, for example, in 'The Good-morrow'. The avowal Donne makes in this poem, 'Only our love hath no decay', is both impossible (all things draw on towards destruction), and inevitable (without such a conviction love cannot exist); the great achievement of 'The Anniversarie' is that in it Donne is able to find a point of balance between the presumptuous (but wonderfully exhilarating) confidence of 'The Sunne rising', and the almost paralysing loss of confidence felt in the concluding lines of 'The Good-morrow'.

In the opening stanza of 'The Anniversarie' Donne affirms the 'first, last, everlasting day' of their love – 'first' and 'last, as it were denied and overthrown by 'everlasting'. But 'first' and 'last' are not to be dismissed so easily: there was a time when they 'first one another saw', and there will come a time when they have to leave each other 'at last in death'. The thought of death thrusts itself forward in the second stanza:

> Two graves must hide thine and my corse,
> If one might, death were no divorce.

The fact is stated with the utmost simplicity; they will both die, and be buried (in separate graves, so presumably they are not husband and wife). This simplicity looks for a moment like calm acceptance of what is, after all, the common lot of mankind:

> Alas, as well as other Princes, wee,
> (Who Prince enough in one another bee,)

> Must leave at last in death, these eyes, and eares,
> Oft fed with true oathes, and with sweet salt teares;

In his sonnet on the death of his wife ('Since she whome I lovd'), Donne maintains a calm so fixed and severe that the reader can only wonder at the strength of the feeling which is being suppressed, and at the still stronger will which suppresses it; Donne's editor, Helen Gardner, finds the poem at one point 'almost intolerably harsh'. The calm of 'The Anniversarie' is, however, less rigid, and it seems to falter a little as Donne lingers on the felt physical presence of the woman before him, whose sight, taste, touch, will all be lost to him with her death ('these eyes, and eares, / Oft fed with true oathes, and with sweet salt teares'). The last four lines of the stanza are a search for consolation:

> But soules where nothing dwells but love;
> (All other thoughts being inmates) then shall prove
> This, or a love increased there above,
> When bodies to their graves, soules from their graves
> remove.

These lines, like those which conclude 'The Good-morrow', are not entirely clear, and in both cases the confusion arises for much the same reasons. Donne's argument seems to be that love alone 'dwells' in their souls, while their 'other thoughts' are merely 'inmates': that is, passing thoughts, or thoughts which are present in their souls without properly belonging to them. Death will dislodge these 'inmates' from their souls, and this will leave the lovers free to enjoy 'a love increased there above'. Accordingly, death can be seen as providing a means of release from the limitations of life. No doubt this is one way of coming to terms with the fact of death, but it does not carry much conviction in the poem, partly because the distinction between dwelling and being an inmate seems somewhat flimsy and uncertain, and partly because Donne is so obviously not content to regard the woman's body as no more than the grave of her soul – 'these eyes, and eares' are too intimately known, too precious to him, for such a piece of piety to afford any genuine consolation. The religious argument is brought in to buttress the lovers' claims to an 'everlasting day' of shared love, but the effect of the stanza as a whole is to suggest once again the intensity with which Donne fears the everlasting night of utter separateness.

The third stanza begins as if John Donne is planning to build upon the unstable foundations of the second, but just as it seems he has gained his point, the argument is unexpectedly dropped, as though the support it offered were no longer what was needed:

> And then wee shall be throughly blest,
> But wee no more, then all the rest;

They will be completely happy ('throughly blest') in the next world, but that will be 'then' and 'there above', and all the evidence of the second stanza is that the lovers are unwilling to set aside the happiness available to them here and now, in this world. Moreover, 'there above' the lovers will be 'no more, than all the rest'; they will have lost their sense of being peculiarly and supremely blessed in their love. It is not so in this world:

> Here upon earth, we'are Kings, and none but wee
> Can be such Kings, nor of such subjects bee.

– they alone can be Kings over such subjects as themselves, and they alone can be subjects under such Kings as each other. There is more assurance here than in the second stanza – they are 'Kings' now, not merely 'Prince enough in one another' ('Prince enough': that is, not really Princes at all) – but this is still far removed from the exuberance and recklessness of 'The Sunne rising'. The assertion of the lovers' supremacy is made to include the admission that theirs is, after all, a kingdom of only two – which is modest indeed, beside 'She'is all States, and all Princes, I, / Nothing else is' – and Donne pauses to consider the grimmer implications of a royalty to be enjoyed 'Here upon earth':

> Who is so safe as wee? where none can doe
> Treason to us, except one of us two.

'*Except one of us two*': 'treason' may cut short the royal life extended to each of them by their mutual love. He may betray her; or she may betray him. This chilling thought, like the fear of their eventual divorce in death, has also to be acknowledged between them.

This is the critical moment in the poem. They could face 'destruction' together, but the prospect of love's 'decay' can only come between them, compelling them against their wills to 'watch … one another out of feare' ('The Good-morrow'). The thought cannot be simply denied, because there are true as well as false fears in love, and to insist otherwise would itself be false; but, whether true or false, such fears are demeaning, and to give way to them, to allow them to take hold over their imaginations, would be to dishonour their status as lovers. Donne meets the crisis with memorable dignity:

> True and false feares let us refraine,
> Let us love nobly, and live, and adde againe
> Yeares and yeares unto yeares, till we attaine
> To write threescore: this is the second of our raigne.

With these lines the inevitable limitations of human life are finally accepted, but accepted bravely. They cannot banish their fears of death or betrayal, because such fears are among the ordinary conditions of our existence, but they can 'refraine' them, keep them under control. To do so will be to 'love nobly': for what could be more ignoble for them than to live in continual fear of some future act of infidelity? Only by refusing to be deterred by fear can they make good their pretensions to royalty in love, and therefore 'live': that is, embrace their happiness here upon earth, rather than wait in timorous expectation of happiness in heaven. If their love cannot in truth be endless, they can still 'attaine / To write threescore', and thereby achieve a triumph not over time but in time. Instead of being daunted by the passing of the years, they will use them as the measure of their fulfilment: 'this is the second of our raigne'.

All this is markedly different from the claims advanced in the first stanza. Their initial aspiration was towards an 'everlasting day' of love, floating free of yesterdays and tomorrows, but this has been gradually let go during the course of the poem: the lovers who began by denying time end by resolving to immerse themselves in it to the full, adding 'Yeares and yeares unto yeares'. But while the original claim has been surrendered, the poem has brought them to a fuller realisation of what can justly be celebrated in a poem about an anniversary: the nobility of a love enjoyed here in the world where they 'first one another saw'.

Part five

Background

John Donne

The life of John Donne is full of fascination for the modern student, for in its mingling of promise and uncertainty Donne's career was typical of his age. He was born in 1572, the third of six children. His father, a successful London merchant, died when Donne was four years old; his mother Elizabeth, a daughter of the writer John Heywood (?1497–?1580), died only two months before Donne's own death in 1631. Both of his parents were Roman Catholics, at a time when members of that faith were coming under increasing pressure to conform to the teaching and practice of the newly established Church of England. Some members of Elizabeth Heywood's family, including her father, went into exile to escape persecution; one of her uncles was executed in 1574; her brother Jasper, a Catholic activist was arrested and banished in the early 1580s; one of her sons was to die in prison in the 1590s. Donne was later to claim with some justice that no family had 'suffered more in their persons and fortunes' for following the Roman Catholic faith than had his own.

Donne was educated privately at first, almost certainly by Catholic tutors, until in 1584, at the age of twelve, he was sent to Oxford. This haste is understandable. At the age of sixteen all university students were required to swear an Oath of Supremacy, acknowledging the position of Elizabeth I (who reigned from 1558 to 1603) as head of the Church in England, and no Catholic could admit Elizabeth's right to an authority also claimed by the Pope. Donne was debarred, as a Catholic, from taking a degree. He was probably at Cambridge in 1588–9, and then may well have travelled abroad, perhaps seeing some military service, before returning to London to enter first Thavies Inn and then Lincoln's Inn as a student of law in 1591. Donne was following the usual path for a young man seeking a political or diplomatic career.

London in the 1590s was the city where Shakespeare was about to make his name. It was, then as now, the centre of literary and intellectual life in England, and Donne naturally responded to the excitements of the city. One contemporary, Richard Baker, described him as 'a great visiter of ladies, a great frequenter of plays, a great writer of conceited verses' ('conceited' here means that the poems were intellectually complicated and ingenious). To this early period belong the *Elegies* and the *Satires*, and probably some of the *Songs and Sonets*, none of the poems printed as yet, but circulated in manuscript among friends. An awareness of this audience of friends is apparent in the tone of much of this early verse, where Donne is deliberately irreverent and unconventional. It is – almost – the kind of poetry that confirms Richard Baker's account of him, as a brilliant young man about town.

Baker's picture, however, is incomplete. Izaac Walton (1593–1683), Donne's earliest biographer, records that at this time Donne was 'unresolved' about his religious position. Donne's difficulties must have been acute. If he remained loyal to his Catholic faith he would have to be prepared to surrender the chance of a successful career. The alternative was hardly more attractive: to overthrow his early training, and to abandon the faith for which three generations of his family had suffered exile and even death. Donne rose every morning at four and studied until ten in the attempt to come to a decision which would satisfy the claims of his conscience and his intellect; in later years he could claim to have 'surveyed and digested' all the points in dispute between the Churches of Rome and England. The year 1593 perhaps brought him to a crisis, for in that year a Catholic priest was found in the rooms of Donne's brother and fellow-student, Henry; the unlucky priest was hanged, disembowelled and quartered, and Henry died in prison of gaol fever. Was Donne to see his own life come to so little? His doubts and hesitations are still apparent in the third of his *Satires* ('Kind pity chokes my spleen'), but by 1595, when his mother left her homeland to go into a voluntary exile with her third husband, Donne had probably made the decision to forsake the Church of Rome: at what cost to himself we can only guess.

In 1596 Donne sailed to Cadiz as a gentleman adventurer with the Earl of Essex (1565–1601) and Walter Raleigh (?1552–1618) in their successful venture against the Spanish, and the following year he sailed again in the less successful 'Islands' voyage to the Azores. Then, in 1597 or 1598, he entered the service of Sir Thomas Egerton

(?1540–1617), Lord Keeper of England, as his chief secretary. Sir Thomas was impressed by the young man, and in 1601 his political influence saw Donne returned as Member of Parliament for Brackley. At the age of twenty-nine, Donne seemed to have every prospect of winning fortune and distinction.

By the end of 1601 a single act had destroyed these bright prospects. Since 1596 Egerton had acted as guardian to Ann More, whose father, Sir George More (1553–1632), was later to become Lieutenant of the Tower of London. Donne and Ann fell in love, and were married without the consent of either father or guardian, thus breaking both canon and civil law. Sir George was outraged, and had Donne committed to prison. He was soon released, and Sir George was unable to have the marriage annulled, but Donne was dismissed from his position as Egerton's secretary. Under these circumstances he was unlikely to find another patron, and he and his young wife (she was then seventeen) moved a short distance from London to manage as best they could. Their situation was summed up in a **punning epigram**: 'Donne, Anne Donne, undone'.

For a time no doubt they were happy enough just to be together, and some of the *Songs and Sonets* portraying satisfied love (for example, 'The Sunne rising') may well date from this period. Sir George was eventually persuaded to accept the situation, and this helped to ease their financial difficulties as their family increased almost year by year. But Donne began to grow restless. He applied desperately to a succession of possible patrons, but was unable to secure a new state appointment. His health began to deteriorate, and he was seriously ill in 1608–9. It was at this time that he wrote his learned treatise in justification of suicide, *Biathanatos*, which perhaps suggests the way his thoughts were turning, and many of the *Divine Poems*. Among these the most memorable are the sonnets known as the *Divine Meditations*, and in particular those in which Donne meditates on the themes of sin and judgement. The cast of his mind was changing.

He continued to study intensively, and possibly put his reading to use by assisting Thomas Morton (1564–1659) in a new bout of polemical writings against the Church of Rome. Still hoping to find a career outside the Church, Donne declined Morton's invitation to enter the Church on the grounds that he was not worthy, but he continued to take part in the controversies, publishing *Pseudo-Martyr* in 1610 and in 1611 *Ignatius His Conclave*. Meanwhile, he continued to seek a patron who would help him to some state employment. He already knew Sir Robert Drury (1575–1615), and when Drury's daughter Elizabeth died in 1610, Donne took advantage of the occasion to write a funeral poem for her, published in 1611. 'An Anatomy of the World (The First Anniversary)' pleased Sir Robert more than it did Donne's fellow poet Ben Jonson, who thought its praise of the dead girl blasphemous, and Donne accompanied the Drury family on a tour to France, Germany and Belgium in 1611–12. (According to Izaac Walton it was before this long journey that Donne wrote for his wife the 'Valediction: forbidding mourning'.) Donne had by now a number of influential friends such as Sir Robert, but although he was again briefly a member of Parliament in 1614, he remained without regular state employment; he wrote in a letter that 'no man attends court fortunes with more impatience than I do'. He finally gave up his political ambitions, and in January 1615 was ordained. At the command of King James he was made an honorary Doctor of Divinity at Cambridge; for a time he was a royal chaplain; and then, in 1616, he was appointed Divinity Reader at Lincoln's Inn. He remained there until 1621, when he was elected Dean of St Paul's Cathedral, the post he held until his death ten years later.

In this last period of his life Donne achieved the distinction he had desired for so long, as he became the most eminent preacher of his generation. But these last years too were marked by sorrow and distress. In 1617 his wife, pregnant for the twelfth time in only sixteen years, died a few days after giving birth to a still-born child. Donne was thus left with seven surviving children to care for, but he never remarried. His own health was still uncertain, and in 1623 he came near to death with a relapsing fever. This illness prompted one of the finest of his religious poems, the 'Hymn to God the Father', and one of the most moving of his prose works, the *Devotions upon Emergent Occasions*, in which work more than in any other is revealed the preoccupation with death which marks much of Donne's writing in the latter half of his life.

In 1630, again seriously ill, Donne made his will, and in February 1631 he preached his last sermon at court, published posthumously as 'Death's Duel'. Izaac Walton recorded that Donne's ill-health was so apparent in his voice and manner that those who heard him believed he had preached his own funeral sermon. He continued to prepare himself for death: almost his last act was to design the monument which was to stand over his grave in St Paul's Cathedral. For this he had made a sketch of himself in his shroud, eyes closed and body half-crouched, which he kept by his bed in the last days to remind himself of what he was soon to become. The statue carved from this portrait survived the Great Fire of 1666 and still stands in the rebuilt cathedral.

John Donne died, aged fifty-nine, on 31 March 1631. The first edition of his poems was printed two years later. For two hundred and fifty years his reputation as a poet was uncertain, though he always had admiring readers: it is only in the present century that he has been generally acknowledged as one of the major poets in English.

HISTORICAL AND RELIGIOUS BACKGROUND

At the beginning of the sixteenth century Europe was ruled by kings, and the culture and the forms of government in England as elsewhere had been largely shaped by the Church of Rome. In 1534, under Henry VIII, England made the break from Rome; by the close of the century it became clear that this break was irreversible, and the extent to which the old culture had given way to new patterns of thought and feeling was already beginning to be felt. With the accession of the Stuart kings, James I and then Charles I, it became apparent that the impetus for change would lead to demands for a new form of government: government, ultimately, by the consent of those governed, instead of government according to the will of the sovereign. Donne was only indirectly concerned with this more narrowly political development, but the religious controversies of the century may fairly be said to have moulded both his private and his public life; and, like other major writers of his time, he was aware of and troubled by the shift of thought and feeling which became apparent in the 1590s, a shift from an Elizabethan world which looked back to a medieval past to a Jacobean world looking forward to our own times.

By the end of the fifteenth century there was widespread agreement that the Church in Western Europe stood in need of reform, although the course and character of what we now know as the Reformation naturally varied from country to country. The crucial factor in England was Henry VIII's need for an annulment of his first marriage, and his inability to obtain it from the Pope. The deadlock was broken in 1534, when the Act of Supremacy declared Henry the Supreme Head of a Church of England independent of Rome. The first decisive step of the English Reformation had been taken, and taken, in effect, in the interests of national government. There was no call to the faithful to examine their souls, nor was there any intention to challenge long cherished ritual or dogma. Henry wanted to preserve unity and stability, and that, he believed, was best done by maintaining as much as possible of the traditional teaching. But individual consciences were stirred by theological arguments carried on elsewhere in Europe by men such as Martin Luther (1483–1546) and John Calvin (1509–64). Soon Henry found himself sending to the stake not only those Catholics who remained loyal to the Pope, but also Protestants who demanded a more radical break from Rome. Had he lived, Henry would probably have been obliged to recognise that the cause of national unity would be better served by more reform than by more burnings.

Under Edward VI, Henry's successor, the reforming party began to establish Protestantism in England. The clergy were allowed to marry, Protestant printers were allowed more freedom, and in 1549 the Act of Uniformity abolished the old Latin mass and instituted a new liturgy as the legal form of worship. These changes were gradual, designed to suit a people who disliked foreign authority and wanted a simpler form of worship, but yet did not wish to depart completely from the old ways. But if England under Edward VI was not yet a genuinely Protestant nation the reign of Mary (1553–8) came near to making it one. Mary was an impassioned Catholic, who hoped to undo all that had been done in twenty years of reform, and to re-establish the authority of the Pope in England. With patience and political intelligence she might have been successful, but she possessed neither. In her short and unhappy reign she burned three hundred Protestants, and ensured that her Church would be identified in English minds for years to come with the idea of tyranny.

Elizabeth I inherited a difficult situation. It is impossible to be certain what her own religious ideas were; what is clear is that, like her father, she was determined to secure national unity, and saw the Church of England as one means to that end. A new Act of Supremacy was passed in 1559, the English Prayer Book was restored, and those who refused to attend services in the Church of England became liable to fines. In practice there was at first a measure of religious toleration: Elizabeth had no wish, in her own memorable phrase, to 'make windows into men's souls', and a show of conformity was usually enough to secure freedom from persecution. Unfortunately this position proved hard to maintain. In 1569 Elizabeth had to put down a rebellion in the North of England, which had mainly Catholic support, and another Catholic plot against her was uncovered in 1571. In 1570 she was excommunicated by the Pope, who later let it be known that it could not be thought a sin to assassinate an excommunicated monarch. Elizabeth's ministers were bound to respond by questioning the loyalty of English Catholics. Penalties for non-attendance at Church services were increased, publishing of seditious books was made an offence punishable by death, and Catholic missionaries were expelled or executed. By the end of the reign, about two hundred Catholics had been put to death, nominally for treason, but in practice for their faith.

Elizabeth's Church was also being challenged from within. Many Protestants who had gone into exile during Mary's reign had come under the influence of John Calvin. Calvinist theology held that God had predestined the spiritual fate of every human being. Those whom God had elected were to be saved, the rest were to be damned. There could be no appeal: salvation could not be earned by sincere faith or by upright conduct, nor could it be awarded by the churches. For this black-and-white theology moderation had little to recommend it, and English Calvinists became known as Puritans from their demand that the Elizabethan Church be further reformed, or purified. The Puritans attacked the theology of the Prayer Book, and they also challenged the position of the bishops in the Church. It was this that convinced Elizabeth that they were a 'sect of perilous consequence': it could only be a short step from attacking her bishops to attacking her right to appoint them. From 1583 onwards Elizabeth's Archbishop, John Whitgift (1530–1604), led a campaign against the Puritans, and from the late 1580s Puritan activists, like their Catholic opponents, risked exile or execution.

Both James I and Charles I shared Elizabeth's fears of the Puritans, who were becoming increasingly powerful in the universities and in Parliament, and both gave full support to the anti-Puritan party, known as Laudians after their most eminent bishop, William Laud (1573–1645), in the campaign to establish stricter uniformity in the Church. Under Elizabeth, Puritan objections to the customs and rituals of the Church of England had not been sharp enough to prevent many of them from continuing to worship in it, but the Laudians began to re-introduce ideas and practices that seemed to the Puritans a revival of Romanism and a betrayal of the Reformation. In 1622 clergy below the level of dean or bishop were forbidden to discuss the doctrines of election and predestination so important to the Puritans, and clergy of all degrees were forbidden to 'meddle' with matters of state. In 1624 it was made an offence to publish any book dealing with religion or church organisation without official approval. (There is some evidence in Donne's sermons of the 1620s to suggest that his sympathies were with the Laudians in these measures.)

It was becoming clear that these divisions were not to be healed peaceably; the moderation of Elizabeth's Church was a thing of the past. For more than a century, controversy over matters of religious belief and practice had merged with political issues; now, those who wished for further reform within the Church found themselves increasingly committed to a direct struggle against the monarchy. In 1642, just over ten years after John Donne's death, England was plunged again into years of civil war.

LITERARY AND INTELLECTUAL BACKGROUND

Significant changes in the patterns of thought and feeling in a society usually make themselves felt only gradually, over a period of several generations. Nonetheless, literary historians find evidence of a decisive shift of outlook and sensibility in England in the late 1590s. The poetry of Sir Philip Sidney (1554–86) and Edmund Spenser (?1552–99) seems to belong to one age; most of the work of Donne, of Shakespeare (1564–1616), and of Ben Jonson (1572–1637) seems to belong to another. A summary but convenient way to describe this difference is to suggest that the earlier writers could accept relatively, comfortably what modern scholars have sometimes called 'the Elizabethan world picture', while the later writers, responding to a wide variety of unsettling influences, were unable to do so.

The Elizabethan world picture emphasised above all else the principle of order: an order appointed by God and operating throughout the whole of creation. In the natural world the principle of order was understood in terms of a hierarchy, as a continuous 'chain of being' ascending from mere inert matter up to God. The central link of this chain was formed by man, connected by his mortal body to the animals, vegetable life and inanimate matter below him, and by his immortal soul to the various degrees of angels ranged above him. Every link in the chain played some part in the divine purpose, and each was related in some way to man and man's activities.

Man was also to be found at the centre of the universe as a whole. This was conceived as a vast system of concentric spheres carrying the moon, the sun, the planets and the stars, all revolving in orbit around the earth. Here too could be found the principle of a divinely-established hierarchy connecting man to his Creator, since it was supposed that the material of which each of the various heavenly bodies was made increased in purity in proportion to its distance from the earth, all the way up to the outermost sphere, called the empyrean, which was the abode of God.

A further principle of order was revealed in a complicated system of analogies known as 'correspondences'. These worked on many different levels. The order evident in the universe was echoed in the corresponding order of the state, where the sovereign was at the centre and each individual was assigned to his own proper social level or 'sphere'; the state in its turn could be seen as an organic unity (called 'the Body Politic'), corresponding to man himself ('the Body Natural'); while man could be seen as a little world, or 'microcosm', which followed the same principles of organisation as those which existed in the whole universe, or 'macrocosm'. The theory of the four 'humours', important in Elizabethan medicine and psychology, is based on this idea of correspondences: just as everything in the universe is composed of different combinations of the four elements, fire, air, earth and water, so each human temperament must be composed of different combinations of the four corresponding humours, choler, blood, black bile and phlegm. The excess of any one of these humours caused ill-health; the remedy was to restore the proper balance, or order.

It was reassuring to believe that the universe was bound together by an infinite series of correspondences and parallels, and this conviction was, understandably, not to be overthrown at once. However, there were a number of factors at work to weaken it during the sixteenth century. The most far-reaching of these, ultimately, was the development of modern experimental science. Medieval and Elizabethan scientists sought to explain natural events by reference to the divine purpose: for example, the appearance of a comet was taken to reveal some disorder in the heavens, and was accordingly interpreted as a message from God to man, a warning to him of some equivalent disorder threatening the human community. The new science, however, was not concerned to illustrate the divine purpose, but to understand the working of natural laws: the appearance of a comet prompted the seventeenth-century scientists to observe its path, and to try to predict the date of its return. In effect, where the old science had allowed religious belief to overlap with rational inquiry, the new science distinguished between them. In making this distinction, the new scientists were necessarily challenging the old conception of the universe as centred on man, and as governed throughout by a divinely appointed principle of order. Two examples will serve to show how great the impact of this challenge was to be.

The first example comes quite directly from the work of the scientists. One of the outstanding achievements of the new scientific methods was to establish that the earth and the other planets revolved in orbit around the sun. This was both literally and metaphorically to displace man from the centre of creation. In repudiating the ideas of earlier theorists, the new astronomers inevitably came into conflict with the traditional teaching of the Church. The old outlook won a temporary victory over the new in 1633 when the Inquisition, acting on behalf of the Church, compelled Galileo Galilei (1564–1642), the greatest scientist of the age, to reject the new theory as heretical, and for much of the seventeenth century it remained true, in Donne's words, that 'new Philosophy calls all in doubt'. But eventually the doubts were settled, and settled on the side of the scientists. Science, in effect, had won from the Church the authority to define the shape and pattern of the universe.

The second example comes from the writings of Niccolo Machiavelli (1469–1527), which effectively began what we now know as political science. Medieval theorists had limited their discussions to such topics as the divine origin of the state, and the principle of hierarchy within it. Machiavelli simply ignored these topics as fanciful and irrelevant; he wanted to analyse the real nature of power in the states he saw being newly forged around him in Italy – states created not by God but by men, and maintained by force and political cunning. In 1513, in *The Prince*, Machiavelli produced what was virtually a handbook of the ways in which political power could be won and held, and he did so without regard to the question of the divine purpose. He was well aware that he was doing something new. In chapter 15 he explains bluntly that his intention is to 'present things as they really are in fact', unlike those earlier writers who had been content to describe 'imaginary republics and princedoms, which never did nor can exist in the real world'. Machiavelli, it may be said, intended to study political movements in the same scientific spirit as Galileo, a century later, was to study the movements of falling objects.

It was this scientific spirit that Francis Bacon was applauding when he wrote, in 1623, that we are all of us indebted 'to Machiavelli and other writers of that class, who openly and unfeignedly describe what men do, and not what they ought to do'. Bacon (1561–1626) was the most influential English spokesman for the new scientific methods, especially in *The Advancement of Learning* (1605). He argued that soundly based scientific knowledge would lead to technical mastery over the world of nature, and that this would be to 'the use and benefit of man'. Many of his contemporaries were less optimistic. What Bacon welcomed as an escape from the limitations of outmoded patterns of thought, they feared as a challenge to the old picture of the world as orderly, unified and centred on man. There was, after all, nothing reassuring in the natural world as described by Galileo, or in the political world as interpreted by Machiavelli. Many factors contributed to the mood of anxiety in England at the close of the sixteenth century – the old age of the childless Queen Elizabeth brought with it a climate of economic and political instability – but the gradual breakdown of the inherited world picture seems to have been the underlying cause of the scepticism and uncertainty that characterise so much of the literature of the period.

The fullest expression of this mood of anxiety is to be found in the work of the dramatists. Shakespeare in particular was clearly preoccupied at this time with a sense of the discrepancy between 'what men do' and 'what they ought to do', and in *Troilus and Cressida* (1602) – a play which may well have been written for the Inns of Court where Donne had been a student a few years earlier – he provided a profound illustration of the new scepticism. The action of the play takes place against the background of the wars between the Greeks and the Trojans. A typical episode is one in which Ulysses, one of the Greek leaders, apparently asserts the familiar Elizabethan ideas of order and hierarchy. In a long speech (1.3.75–137) he argues that 'the heavens themselves, the planets, and this centre' (that is, the earth) all observe 'degree, priority, and place', and that these principles must be observed throughout the human community as well. If at any point the principle of degree is 'shaked', argues Ulysses, then the whole world will fall into chaos and anarchy. These fine words meet with general approval, but nonetheless they have no influence at all on the way the Greeks conduct the war, and indeed a moment later Ulysses himself proposes a plot which will involve the violation of the principle of degree he has just set forth (the hero Achilles is to be downgraded, and the foolish Ajax advanced in his place). The rest of the action of the play consists mainly of a series of increasingly brutal betrayals in love and war. Not surprisingly, *Troilus and Cressida* has been seen as Shakespeare's dramatisation of the collapse of traditional values – love, honour, loyalty – as a result of the disintegration of the world picture so eloquently described, and then abandoned, by Ulysses.

It would, however, be misleading to suggest that John Donne and Shakespeare and all the writers contemporary with them could be divided neatly into those who wholly opposed, and those who wholly welcomed, the emergence of the new sceptical outlook. That the situation was not so simple as this is clear both from the work of the **satirists**, and from what happened to the love poetry of the period. In each case, poems by Donne supply the most instructive examples.

The sudden fashion for satire in the 1590s was another sign of the changing mood of the times. Not only Donne, but also Thomas Lodge (?1558–1625), Joseph Hall (1574–1656), and John Marston (?1575–1634) published verse satires during this decade. The satirists saw it as their task to expose and condemn what Marston called the 'soul-polluting beastliness' of the age (in *The Scourge of Villainy*, 1598), and much of their writing was both bitter and abusive. But it could hardly be said that their work reveals a cowed or defeated state of mind: on the contrary, the satirists responded to life in London at the turn of the century with almost endless energy. Their work abounds in details of manners, fashions and customs, and lively accounts of the disreputable behaviour of courtiers, prostitutes, former soldiers, and (especially) lawyers. The first of Donne's Satyres ('Away thou fondling motley humourist') possesses this energy in full measure. The poem opens with Donne telling the friend who calls on him that he prefers the quiet company of his books to the noise and bustle out of doors. However, it soon becomes evident that he is delighted to have been interrupted, and his running commentary on all that they see in the streets establishes the poet as far more knowing about the ways of the town than his supposedly 'wild' and frivolous companion. The enthusiasm here for the satirist's task, and the abundance of entertaining detail, suggests that a sceptical awareness of the gulf between 'what men do' and 'what they ought to do' was not necessarily a barrier to a healthy and, indeed, exhilarating appetite for life in all its variety.

The last decade of the sixteenth century saw a renewal of vigour in the love poetry of the age. There had always been many fine Elizabethan love poems, but many more were both competent and dull:

> Smooth are thy looks, so is the deepest stream;
> Soft are thy lips, so is the swallowing sand;
> Fair is thy sight, but like unto a dream;
> Sweet is thy promise, but it will not stand.
> Smooth, soft, fair, sweet, to them that lightly touch;
> Rough, hard, foul, sour to them that take too much.
>
> Thy looks so smooth have driven away my sight,
> Who would have thought that hooks could be so hid?
> Thy lips so soft have fretted my delight,
> Before I once suspected that they did.
> Thy face so fair hath burnt me with desire,
> Thy words so sweet were bellows for the fire.

> And yet I love the looks that made me blind,
> And like to kiss the lips that fret my life,
> In heat of fire an ease of heat I find,
> And greatest peace of mind in greatest strife,
> That if my choice were now to make again,
> I would not have this joy without this pain.

This poem, published anonymously in 1602, is in the tradition of English **Petrarchism**, so called after the Italian poet Francesco Petrarca (1304–74), many of whose poems were translated into English during the sixteenth century. This tradition is distinguished by the elaborate and extravagant comparisons applied to the lady, who is as cold and remote as she is beautiful, and to the despairs of the lover, presented as her devoted and suffering servant. Donne's restless and sceptical mind had little use for such a convention, and in the *Elegies* of the 1590s, as in the *Songs and Sonets*, the traditions of Petrarchism are discarded. In most of these poems the lady is no longer remote, but in the bedroom, and the poet no longer a passive servant but an active lover. The possibility of so natural and desirable a conclusion to their sufferings seems hardly to have occurred to the Petrarchan poets.

The immediate consequence of this dismissal of Petrarchism is that John Donne's love poetry shows the same appetite and energy that we find in the satirists:

> Licence my roving hands, and let them goe
> Behind, before, above, between, below
>
> ...
>
> How blest am I in this discovering thee. (Elegie: 'To his Mistress going to Bed')

The interest here is very precisely in 'what men do', and not in what ought to be done or felt by the idealised lovers of the Petrarchan convention. In Donne's love poems, as in Shakespeare's *Sonnets* of roughly the same period, the reader is conscious that the realities of human sexual experience are never far away. This is clearly not the case with 'Smooth are thy looks', in which such words as 'peace' and 'strife', 'joy' and 'pain', do not direct us to the real nature of sexual experience, but remain merely words to be shuffled about to suit the symmetries of the poem:

> Smooth, soft, fair, sweet, to them that lightly touch;
> Rough, hard, foul, sour to them that take too much.

Such symmetries are mildly pleasing, and suggest a world that is orderly and harmonious; they belong to what has been described above as the 'Elizabethan world picture'. Donne's poetry is of quite another kind, and implies a quite different account of reality. The recurrent theme of the *Songs and Sonets* is the place of human love not in the timeless and ideal world of Petrarchan poetry, but in a world vulnerable to change and death. In this real world, love may be present under many aspects – promiscuity, hopeless adoration, bitter disillusionment, cheerful cynicism, tender intimacy – and Donne's love poetry encompasses all of these. In this respect, what F.R. Leavis wrote in *Revaluation* (Chatto & Windus) in 1936 is still true: Donne is 'obviously a living poet in the most important sense'. Perhaps, then, there is no better way to recommend Donne to the modern reader than to say that it is the peace and strife, the joys and pains, of the world we know that are evoked and examined in such poems as 'The Sunne rising', 'Love's Alchymie', and 'The Anniversarie'.

PART SIX

CRITICAL HISTORY AND FURTHER READING

The first phases in the debate about John Donne's achievement as a poet have been outlined earlier in this Note (see Critical Approaches). Donne's poetry was published for the first time in 1633. Within a decade, the Civil War had begun, and by the time Charles II came to the throne in 1660, literary fashions had changed. The theatres had been closed under the Puritans, interrupting one important element in the native literary tradition; meanwhile, writers who had been in exile abroad had come under the influence of French ideas and manners. Writers and readers in the later seventeenth century found Donne's verse powerful, but too irregular; Alexander Pope even rewrote the *Satyres* in a smoother, less abrasive style, while Samuel Johnson thought it was possible to recognise Donne's verse as verse only by counting syllables. Donne was occasionally admired, but almost always treated as odd and, typically, approached through such labels as '**metaphysical**'. It has been part of the aim of this Note to emphasise Donne's centrality, rather than his oddity.

Donne's poetry always attracted admirers. The **Romantic** poet and critic Samuel Taylor Coleridge was fascinated by his intellectual complexity. Romantic critics were often drawn towards strong, individual personalities, and Donne was nothing if not individual, but Coleridge was also fascinated by many of the more obscure texts Donne had read. But while Coleridge, who was a famous conversationalist, has some interesting remarks on Donne (those on his **rhythm** have been quoted earlier) he made no effort to write a systematic account of his work. Much the same is true of Robert Browning, a generation later. We know that Browning read Donne, and the dramatic situations and rhythmic energy of his poetry owe something to Donne's influence: for example, each had the knack of beginning a poem with a striking phrase (one of Browning's earliest monologues begins with the all but unpronounceable 'G-r-r-r'), and, more importantly, each found a way to make the reader conscious of the silent partner as the poem develops only one side of a conversation.

But, like the Romantics, Victorian readers typically showed little interest in English poetry between Shakespeare and Milton, and in neither period do we find a significant account of Donne as a poet.

JOHN DONNE IN THE TWENTIETH CENTURY

NEW CRITICAL APPROACHES

It was then in the early twentieth century that Donne acquired his reputation as a major poet. A key figure here was the poet T.S. Eliot. In two brief essays, on 'The Metaphysical Poets' and 'Andrew Marvell' (reprinted in T.S. Eliot, *Selected Essays*, Faber, London, 1932), Eliot challenged Johnson's view that '**wit**' is at odds with poetic seriousness. Eliot's own poetry was, like Donne's, learned, witty, and difficult, and, again like Donne's, it was equally a poetry of ideas and of emotion. Eliot's famous description, in 'The Love Song of J. Alfred Prufrock', of the evening 'spread out against the sky / Like a patient etherised upon a table', is not precisely a **conceit,** in that the point of comparison cannot be demonstrated logically in the way that Donne's comparison of parted lovers to a pair of compasses can be – Eliot's line works by association and suggestion, rather than by logical parallel – but it does share something of Donne's willingness to look in strange places for his ideas and illustrations. If Eliot is not here influenced by Donne, we can at least see why he might be interested in him. An influential essay by F. R. Leavis, 'The Line of Wit' (in *Revaluation*, Chatto & Windus, London, 1936), developed Eliot's arguments. In effect, both writers were seeking to rewrite the history of English literature in a way that connected modern experiments in poetry with the traditions of Shakespeare and Donne.

The essays by Eliot and Leavis helped set the tone for the university study of Donne. At the least profound level, Donne's poems are complex enough to justify devoting an hour-long class to their analysis; in other words, they can be used to provide a training in the skills of close reading. The practise of these skills was associated with what became known as the **New Criticism**. New Critical readings tended to treat the poem as a self-contained artefact, concentrating on the words on the page, and setting aside biographical or historical considerations. This approach was most rewarding when used on poems which were marked by **irony** and **ambiguity**. References to intention, or biography, like other kinds of historical evidence, were set aside as irrelevant or fallacious. The arguments for this were powerful, if also rather bullying. Those who opposed what they called the **Intentional Fallacy** held (a) that if an effect intended by the poet is realised or accomplished within the poem, there was no need to refer outside the poem for evidence of it – it was, as they liked to put it, 'there' in the poem; and (b) that if an intended effect was not realised in the poem, reference to the author's intention was irrelevant to the words on the page – by definition, the effect was not 'there'.

This is not to suggest that New Criticism was merely technical, without interest in human experience. The poems the New Critics most admired were typically those which brought various opposing moods and ideas into a final coherence. The reader's experience was one of conflict followed by reconciliation, and it is easy to see why this model of how we read could be found attractive, especially against the background of the World War and the conflicts of the Cold War in the 1940s and 1950s. The New Critics may have refused to look at history when debating literary meaning, but their own approach was, inevitably, shaped by the history of their time. It will be evident from the kinds of reading offered in the Extended Commentaries why John Donne's kind of poetry might be seized upon for New Critical readings.

PSYCHOANALYTIC READINGS

We shall return later to the idea of 'coherence' (see **Post-structuralist** Readings). It might be useful first to note two ways of reading Donne which we might have expected to be widely tried, but which in fact have (to date) made little impact.

The first of these is through the techniques of **psychoanalysis**. We know a great deal about the external facts of Donne's life – his family, education, career, marriage and so on – much more than we do about most of his contemporaries. We also have a considerable amount of written material from his own hand: not just the poems, but a variety of religious writings – including pamphlets, meditations written for his private use, and many of his sermons – as well as a treatise in defence of suicide, and a large number of his letters. These documents, taken together, suggest a man of deep contradictions. To take only one example, we cannot be sure whether he left the Catholic faith and accepted the teachings of the Church of England because he was led to do so by his conscience, or whether he chose to do so because his Catholicism stood in the way of his career. It might seem, then, that a psychoanalytic approach to his work would be rewarding, all the more perhaps since the work of Freud in particular was coming to be well-known just as Donne was acquiring his modern reputation. In fact, while many critics have hazarded a guess at Donne's motives, including those which might have remained hidden even from himself, there has been no serious attempt at a psychoanalytic reading.

The critic who has made the most intriguing comments in this line is John Carey, in his *Donne: Life, Mind, and Art* (Faber, London, 1981). Two examples will suggest something of the strengths and limitations of this kind of criticism. Carey notes the sexual bravado of such poems as 'Elegy: To his Mistris Going to Bed', and wonders how far this defiant assertion of his masculinity may have been prompted by Donne's memory of witnessing the torture and execution of Catholic priests, which included their public emasculation. He also comments on the difficulties Donne must have faced in choosing to reject the Catholicism for which so many members of his family had suffered death or exile, and suggests that the preoccupation with change and infidelity which marks many of the *Songs and Sonets* may be understood as the displacement of Donne's guilt at what some of his friends and family must have considered his act of betrayal.

How should we respond to these suggestions? One reply might be that we have to note, as Carey himself does, that we cannot come to a conclusion about the reality of motives of which Donne himself might have been unaware. In its cruder forms, psychoanalytic criticism has sometimes made itself unanswerable: if the reader does not accept the critic's interpretation of *Hamlet* as a play shaped by the **Oedipus complex**, as described by Freud, that is because the reader cannot admit that he too has been shaped by that complex. There is nothing in Carey's position as crude as this, but we might still be unsure what we can do with an interpretation of Donne which neither we, nor Donne himself, could we set him before us, can ever confirm or deny.

The second point to make about this kind of criticism is closely related to the first. If Carey's suggestions are accepted, what does that tell us about the poems? The discussion offered earlier of 'The Anniversarie' presents it as a poem about the way men and women in love wish to use such words as 'for ever', yet know both that they cannot do so (we are mortal, and we change) and that they must do so (only if we have some such faith can we risk ourselves in love). If we take Carey's view that lying behind such a poem is Donne's guilt at his apostasy, this will not turn it into a coded poem about religious betrayal. What it will do, and do usefully, is remind us how our most profound beliefs and feelings in one area of our lives may have been formed in some quite different area. We are much less transparent to ourselves than we would like to believe. But while this is true, and important, it leaves 'The Anniversarie' much as it is.

GENDER READINGS

It has long been a convention in English writing to refer to the reader as 'he' (I have done so deliberately, above, in referring to the Oedipus complex). But readers are both male and female, and the notion of a gendered reading is an attempt to recognise that fact. Since Donne's poems are so often concerned with the relation between men and women, it seems that it might be in this case an important fact, but this too is an approach to Donne which has been less explored than one might expect.

A note first on the term 'gendered reading' rather than 'feminist reading', however much in practice the two have overlapped. The modern feminist movement dates essentially from the late 1960s; feminist literary criticism came soon after. Both, unsurprisingly, have complex and contested histories, and the definitions offered here are presented cautiously. But one might suggest (a) that a feminist must believe, at least, that women have been, and continue to be, systematically disadvantaged on the grounds of their sex, and that this ought not to be so; and (b) that the basis of feminist literary criticism is the recognition that gender has an influence on, if it does not determine, the way books are written, distributed and read. A male critic sympathetic to the feminist claim may feel in response to (a) that women are better judges of the nature and degree of their disadvantage, and better placed to decide how to resist it (the best he can do may often be simply to listen, or to get out of the way); and in response to (b) that men, like women, have genders, and the way men write, or read, as men, is not to taken as the norm, but needs to be the subject of investigation. The term 'gendered reading' is used here to resist the idea that there are gender-free readings of Donne, proposed by men, and gendered readings, proposed by feminists. The issues raised by feminist critics are issues for men as well as for women.

A helpful starting-point for the further investigation of these issues in a reading of Donne is provided by the chapter on 'Gendered Readings' in *New Latitudes*, by Thomas Healy (Edwin Arnold, Suffolk, 1992). Healy quotes and comments on Donne 's lines, 'Oh my America, my new-found-land, / My kingdome, safeliest when with one man man'd' from his 'Elegy: To his Mistris going to Bed'. In Healy's reading the **image** suggests that the woman is a virgin territory, and the man the explorer; she waits passively for him to arrive and claim her, take possession of her treasures, even to assign a name to her. The comment that she is 'safeliest when with one man man'd' is interpreted to mean that as a virgin she will be free from sexually transmitted diseases: 'safe', in other words, to Donne. While the poem is ostensibly addressed to the woman, she is not allowed to speak, and while the male speaker refers to 'bonds', as if admitting some form of commitment or obligation, the description of his 'roving hands' suggests a piratical rather than a responsible attitude to their relationship.

The point here is not whether Healy's reading of the poem is the most persuasive (one of Donne's editors, Helen Gardner, thinks that the woman, so far from being a virgin, is at any rate sexually experienced, if not a prostitute), but rather that it opens up questions about how it is to be read. There are clearly questions here for women readers, who may wonder about the role assigned to them in the poem. But there are also questions for male readers, who may wonder how far they wish to identify with the 'male' voice in the poem. Is this poem, in fact, one of the texts which has shaped our sense of what it is to be male or female? And if it is, how might we extend this kind of analysis to such poems as 'The Good-morrow' or 'The Sunne rising', both of which glance at the image of the woman as a territory awaiting discovery and possession?

POST-STRUCTURALIST READINGS

In the discussion of **New Critical** approaches to John Donne, it was suggested that for many readers within this tradition one of the pleasures of poetry, including Donne's, was the sense it gave of varying or conflicting meanings brought together into some kind of coherence. What seems to underlie such a notion is the belief that there exists a 'normal' reader, whose experience both tests and is tested by the poem. Where two or more readers – for example, the members of a tutorial class or seminar – found themselves coming to agreement about a poem, or about the attitude towards sexual or religious experience suggested by the poem, it was natural to conclude that what had been understood was not merely something technical about an arrangement of words, but rather something about the nature of our moral, emotional or intellectual life. This could be seen as a rather more modest form of an idea often expressed in the nineteenth century, that the poet (or novelist) was a source of wisdom, reaching intuitively the kinds of insight which eluded scientists or philosophers. In its revised form, the claim was not so much for the genius of the individual writer, as for the value of the shared understanding of trained readers attending with the utmost care to works of literature.

But it might be argued that the idea of the 'normal' reader, like the idea of a universal truth embodied in a poem, is a comforting myth. In reality, readers are men or women, young or old, black or white, and so on; readers have histories, they live in history, and their experience is as often as not of conflict rather than of coherence. In the past twenty years or so, new critical approaches have emerged which draw attention to the failures of coherence. These are not blamed on the poet; instead, the poem is seen as a kind of battlefield, or 'site' (to use a favourite image), where careful study can see evidence of the contradictions within the age in which the poem was written.

It is again easy to see why Donne's poetry has attracted such readings. To take just one example, it looks back to ideas inherited from medieval Christianity, which see time as unreal, and eternity as the only reality, and at the same time looks forward to what we might think of as the modern sense that fulfilment can come only through an acceptance of time and change. What we see in Donne (it can be argued) is not just one man struggling to come to terms with his personal situation, but the arguments and uncertainties of an age making themselves felt within his writing.

We can see the critical shift being outlined here if we compare Helen Gardner's edition of the *Songs and Sonets* (published in 1965) with an essay by Tilottama Rajan, published in the journal *English Literary History* in 1982. Gardner, on the one hand, proposed a division of the *Songs and Sonets* into an earlier and a later group, with the more cynical or casual poems presumed to have been written earlier, and the more obviously thoughtful ones assigned to a later date. In part the aim of such a grouping is to make both the poems, and the man who wrote them, appear more coherent. It allows us, for example, to speak of Donne's 'development', and it is an easy step from this idea to more contentious ones, such as 'maturity'. Rajan, on the other hand, speculates that Donne deliberately randomised the arrangement of his poems precisely in order to challenge the assumption that the natural human experience is to move steadily onward from error or partial truth on towards a fuller or even complete understanding.

There are other ways in which one can describe these critical shifts. It might be said that Donne and his contemporaries faced the experience of being **decentred** in the physical universe, as the astronomers showed that the earth revolved around the sun, and not the sun and the planets around the earth, while in the late twentieth century many theorists have decentred men and women in the moral universe, by calling into question the very idea of the self. Those who have developed arguments of this kind have often been described, perhaps not very informatively, as post-structuralists. This is a blanket term to cover a variety of positions, which have in common the conviction that meaning is not a 'given', part of the nature of reality, but constructed by conventional frameworks of thought and language. Because these frameworks are themselves historically determined, none of them – including our own – has any final authority. If there is no truth, it makes no sense to discuss Donne's development, if we mean by that his progress towards a true understanding of the nature of things.

But there is no need for the reader of Donne's poetry to address these large issues in order to enjoy the poems. The importance of reading the poems aloud was stressed at the very beginning of this Note. We do not read poetry with the eye only; we also have to speak the poems, to feel them in our own voice. We can make proper distinctions between studying the age in which they were written, the man who wrote them, or the words on the page in front of us; but each of these begins with attending to our own experience as we read. That experience will be shaped by many factors, including whether we are men or women, old or young, or from western or eastern cultures. It will sometimes be pleasurable, sometimes disturbing; it should always be exciting.

Great poems, according to the poet W.H. Auden read us, as much as we read them. The suggestions for further reading which follow have been made with this two-way and challenging process in mind.

FURTHER READING

EDITIONS OF JOHN DONNE'S POETRY

Helen Gardner, ed., *John Donne: The Divine Poems*, Clarendon Press, Oxford, 1952

> The standard scholarly edition, with full textual notes

Helen Gardner, ed., *John Donne: The Elegies and the Songs and Sonets*, Clarendon Press, Oxford, 1965

> The standard scholarly edition of the love poetry, with full textual notes

H.J.C. Grierson, ed., *The Poems of John Donne*, 2 volumes, Clarendon Press, Oxford, 1912

> For forty years the standard edition of John Donne's poems, and still of great value

T. Redpath, ed., *The Songs and Sonets of John Donne*, Methuen, London, 1956

> A full and helpful annotation: now available in a paperback edition

A.J. Smith, ed., *John Donne: The Complete English Poems*, Penguin Books, Harmondsworth, 1971

> The fullest and most fully annotated one-volume edition of the poems. The text is slightly modernised: useful bibliography

BIOGRAPHIES OF JOHN DONNE

A number of the critical studies listed below include some biographical information; the standard life of John Donne is R.C. Bald, *John Donne: A Life*, Clarendon Press, Oxford, 1970.

CRITICAL STUDIES

In an ideal world, the student coming to John Donne for the first time might make his or her way through the following studies in turn, before embarking on any of the more specialised and often highly detailed scholarly discussions:

James Winny, *A Preface to Donne*, Longman, London, 1970; revised, 1981

> This contains much useful information on the life and background, and discussions of a number of poems by John Donne and his contemporaries

C.S. Lewis, 'Donne and Love Poetry in the Seventeenth Century', and Joan Bennett, 'The Love Poetry of John Donne: A Reply to Mr. C.S. Lewis', both originally in J. Dover Wilson, ed., *Seventeenth-Century Studies Presented to Sir Herbert Grierson*, Clarendon Press, Oxford, 1938; also available in W.R. Keast, ed., *Seventeenth-Century English Poetry*, Oxford University Press, New York, 1962

> Lewis's hostile account of John Donne's love poetry is discussed earlier in this Note – see Introduction

Samuel Johnson, 'The Life of Cowley', in J.P. Hardy, ed., *Johnson's Lives of the Poets. A Selection*, Oxford University Press, Oxford, 1971

> Johnson's brief discussion of 'metaphysical poetry' remains the one account of John Donne and his supposed followers that every student of John Donne needs to consider

T.S. Eliot, 'The Metaphysical Poets' and 'Andrew Marvell', both reprinted in T.S. Eliot, *Selected Essays*, Faber, London, 1932; revised edition, 1951

> Eliot challenges Johnson's view that John Donne's 'wit' is incompatible with poetic seriousness in two brief essays; in espousing John Donne, Eliot helped to bring about a revolution in taste which made John Donne one of the most admired of English poets

F.R. Leavis, 'The Line of Wit', in *Revaluation*, Chatto and Windus, London, 1936

> Leavis was one of the first academic critics to develop Eliot's arguments, and *Revaluation* one of the most influential of modern critical studies

Wilbur Sanders, *John Donne's Poetry*, Cambridge University Press, Cambridge, 1971

> Sanders continues the argument between Johnson and Eliot, and in doing so produces perhaps the most sympathetic and persuasive of all the studies of John Donne's love poetry; the discussion of the religious poems is less satisfactory, but still rewarding

J.B. Leishman, *The Monarch of Wit*, Hutchinson, London, 1951

> Leishman's study, though less lively than that of Sanders, covers much of the ground that any student needs to consider

John Carey, *John Donne: Life, Mind, and Art*, Faber, London, 1981

> An ambitious and wide-ranging study, better suited to the student who is already well informed about John Donne; this, with Sanders's book, offers the best and liveliest criticism John Donne has had

Tilottama Rajan, '"Nothing Sooner Broke": Donne's *Songs and Sonets* as Self-Consuming Artifacts', *English Literary History*, 49 (1982), pages 809–28

> This essay is discussed earlier in this Note, as an example of the most recent movements in literary criticism

Gary Waller, *English Poetry of the Sixteenth Century*, Longman, Harlow, 1986

> As the title suggests, this is a broad-based history of English poetry in the period up to and including John Donne, on whose poetry it has a useful and suggestive chapter

P. Cruttwell, *The Shakespearean Moment*, Chatto and Windus, London, 1954, and 'The Love Poetry of John Donne: Pedantique Weeds or Fresh Invention', in M. Bradbury and D. Palmer, eds, *Metaphysical Poetry*, Arnold, London, 1970

> The discussion of John Donne in *The Shakespearean Moment*, as well as the later essay, have the great merit of sending the reader back to the poems with renewed vigour

World events	Author's life	Literary events
		1513 Niccolò Machiavelli, *The Prince*
		1517 Martin Luther, *Ninety-five Theses*
		1529 Martin Luther, *Small Catechism*
1534 Act of Supremacy declares Henry VIII the Supreme Head of a Church of England		
		1535 First English translation of The Bible
1536 Execution of Anne Boleyn		**1536** John Calvin, *Institutes of the Christian Religion*
1538 Pope Paul III excommunicates Henry VIII		
1539 3,000 religious houses destroyed		
1545 First Council of Trent		**1545** John Skelton, *Collyn Clout*
1547 Death of Henry VIII; accession of Edward VI		
1549 Act of Uniformity forbidding Catholic Mass		
1551 Second Council of Trent		
1552 Second Act of Uniformity enforces use of Prayer Book		
1553 Death of Edward VI; Lady Jane Grey rules for 9 days; accession of Catholic Queen Mary; restoration of Catholicism begins		
1554 Act of Supremacy repealed		
1558 Death of Queen Mary; accession of Elizabeth I		
1559 Restoration of Protestantism		
		1564 Births of Shakespeare, Marlow and Galileo

World events	Author's life	Literary events
1569 Catholic rebellion in North of England		
1570 Elizabeth I excommunicated		
	1572 Born into a Catholic Family	
	1574 His great uncle is executed	
	1576 Father dies	
		1579 Edmund Spenser, *The Shepheardes Calendar*
1582 Plague in London		
1584 Revelation of Philip II of Spain's plot to depose Elizabeth I	**1584** Goes to Oxford (age 11)	
1587 Mary Queen of Scots executed; Drake destroys Spanish fleet at Cadiz		
1588 Spanish Armada defeated	**1588-9** Goes to Cambridge	**1588** William Byrd, *Psalms, Sonnets and Songs*
		1589 George Puttenham, *The Art of English Poesy*
		1590 Christopher Marlow, *Tamburlaine (Part 1);* Sir Philip Sidney, *Arcadia;* Edmund Spenser, *Fairie Queen, (Books I-III);* Thomas Lodge, *Rosalynde*
	1591 Becomes a law student	**1591** Sir Philip Sidney, *Astrophel and Stella*
1592 Plague in London	**1592** Is admitted to Lincoln's Inn	**1592** Thomas Kyd, *The Spanish Tragedy*
	1592-6 Probably writes *Satyres*	
1593 Execution of 5 puritans for denying Queen's supremacy	**1593** A Catholic priest is found in his brother's rooms; the brother later dies in gaol	
	1595 Probably makes decision to relinquish Roman Catholic faith and joins Anglican Church	**1595** Sir Philip Sydney, *Defence of Poesy;* William Shakespeare, *Romeo and Juliet*

World events	Author's life	Literary events
1596 Earl of Essex storms Cadiz	**1596** Sails to Cadiz with the Earl of Essex	
	1597 Azores expedition; becomes chief secretary to Sir Thomas Egerton	
1598 Edict of Nantes; death of King Philip II of Spain		**1598** Ben Jonson, *Every Man Out of His Humour;* John Marston, *Certain Satires*
		1599 William Shakespeare, *As You Like It*
		1600 William Shakespeare, *Twelfth Night*
1601 Earl of Essex is executed	**1601** Becomes member of Parliament for Brackley; marries Anne More without consent thus breaking the law; he is committed to prison and dismissed from Sir Thomas Egerton's service	**1601** Ben Jonson, *The Poetaster;* William Shakespeare, *Hamlet*
	1602 Released from prison; lives, without a patron, in London; probably writes many of the *Songs and Sonnets* at this time	
	1602-4 Residence with Sir Francis Wooley at Pyrford; writes *The Progresse of the Soule*	
1603 Death of Elizabeth I; accession of James I of England and VI of Scotland		**1603** Ben Jonson, *The Satyr*
1604 James I rejects puritan petitions at Hampton Court Conference	**1604-7** May be collaborating with Thomas Morton writing anti-Catholic pamphlets under Morton's name	**1604** Christopher Marlowe, *Dr Faustus* printed for the first time; William Shakespeare, *Othello;* John Marston, *The Malcontent*
1605 Gunpowder Plot; severe laws passed against Catholics	**1605-7** Employed by Thomas Morton	**1605** Miguel de Cervantes, *Don Quijoté de la Mancha;* William Shakespeare, *King Lear;* Francis Bacon, *Advancement of Learning*

World events	Author's life	Literary events
	1605-9 Residence at Mitcham	
		1606 Ben Jonson, *Volpone*; William Shakespeare, *Macbeth*
		1607 John Marston, *What You Will*
	1609-18 Writes *Holy Sonnets*	
	1610 *Pseudo-Martyr* published	**1610** Ben Jonson, *The Alchemist*
1611 Authorised version of Bible is published	**1611** *Ignatius His Conclave* published; writes *The First Anniversarie*	**1611** William Shakespeare, *The Tempest*
	1611-12 Accompanies the Drury family on a tour to France, Germany and Belgium	
	1612 'The First Anniversarie' reprinted with 'The Second Anniversarie'	**1612** John Webster, *The White Devil*
	1614 Becomes a member of Parliament again	**1614** Ben Jonson, *Bartholomew Fair;* John Webster, *The Duchess of Malfi*
	1615 Gives up political ambitions and is ordained; becomes an honorary Doctor of Divinity at Cambridge	
	1616 Is appointed Divinity Reader at Lincoln's Inn	**1616** Death of Shakespeare
	1617 His wife dies in childbirth (12th pregnancy)	
1618 Raleigh executed for treason; Thirty Years' War begins in Europe		
	1619-20 With Lord Doncaster's Embassy in Germany	
1620 Pilgrim Fathers set sail in the *Mayflower* for the New World		
	1621 Is elected Dean of St Paul's Cathedral	

World events	Author's life	Literary events
	1623 Nearly dies; writes 'Hymn to God the Father' and *Devotions upon Emergent Occasions*	**1623** Shakespeare's *First Folio* published
1624 Plague in London; war declared against Spain		
1625 Accession of Charles I		
	1626 *V Sermons* published	
		1627 Francis Bacon, *The New Atlantis*
	1631 Delivers the so-called funeral sermon 'Death's Duel'; dies two months later (31 March)	
1633 Galileo censured by the Inquisition	**1633** First edition of *Poems* printed	**1633** George Herbert, *The Temple: Sacred Poems and Private Ejaculations*
		1635 Sir Thomas Browne, *Religio Medici*
	1640 *LXXX Sermons* published	
1642 Outbreak of Civil War		
	1646 *Biathanatos* published	**1646** Sir John Suckling, *Fragmenta Aurea;* Richard Crashaw, *Steps to the Temple*
		1648 Robert Herrick, *Hes perides*
1649 Execution of Charles I	**1649** *Fifty Sermons* published	**1649** Richard Lovelace, *Lucasta: Epodes, Odes, Sonnets, Songs*
	1651 *Letters* and *Essayes in Divinity* published	**1651** Thomas Hobbes, *Leviathan*
		1653 Izaac Walton, *The Compleat Angler, or the Contemplative Man's Recreation*
	1661 *XXVI Sermons* published	
1666 Great Fire of London		
		1667 John Milton, *Paradise Lost*

alliteration the repetition of consonantal sounds (usually at the beginning of a word, and often in successive words) in a piece of writing

ambiguity the capacity of words or phrases to have more than one meaning, or conflicting meanings (see the notes to 'Since she whome I lovd', lines 3–4, for an example in Donne)

analogy a word, thing, idea or story, chosen for the purpose of comparison, which can help to explain whatever it is similar to

assonance the use of the same vowel sounds with different consonants in successive words or stressed syllables e.g. nation and traitor

aubade a poem greeting the dawn, usually with the suggestion of lovers about to part

colloquial/colloquialism the use of the kinds of expression and grammar associated with ordinary, everyday speech rather than formal language

conceit originally equivalent to concept, but in relation to John Donne and some of his contemporaries used to describe an unexpected or improbable comparison between two or more apparently dissimilar things or ideas, generally though not necessarily extended over several lines of verse

couplet a pair of rhymed lines, of any metre

decentre/decentring the process of removing power from some perceived centre of authority. In much post-structuralist criticism, literature itself has been decentred

diction the choice of vocabulary in a literary text; in some periods this has encompassed the whole language (as it seems to do for Donne), while at other times some words have been regarded as available for poetry and others set aside as unsuitable

elegy in modern usage, a poem lamenting the death of (typically) a single person, but in the sixteenth century applied more widely to a reflective poem in a regular metre

epigram any short poem which has a sharp turn of thought or point, be it witty, amusing or satiric

foot in order to work out the metre of a line of verse, it is necessary to divide it into 'feet', which are certain fixed combinations of weakly and strongly stressed syllables into which the line is divided e.g. iamb

free verse verse released from the convention of metre with its regular pattern of stresses and lengths. It is printed in broken-up lines like verse (not continuously like prose) and is often very rhythmical

grammar the way words combine to form sentences; see syntax

half-rhyme an imperfect rhyme

iamb the most frequently used metrical pattern in English verse, consisting of a weak or unstressed syllable followed by a stressed one; in iambic verse, the most common ways to vary the pattern are to add an unstressed syllable (making the line hypermetric, that is, having one syllable beyond the norm for the poem), or to reverse the pattern (usually at the beginning of a line, so that it begins with a stressed syllable)

idiom a phrase or way of expressing something special to a language, sometimes ungrammatical or illogical

image, imagery all the words which refer to objects and qualities which appeal to the senses and feelings; see also metaphor and simile

Intentional fallacy American New Critics introduced this term for what they regarded as the mistaken critical method of judging a literary work according to the author's intentions, whether stated or implied. They argued that the value and meaning of each literary work resides solely in the text itself

irony saying one thing while intending or implying another; often related to ambiguity (see above) as a means of building conflict or uncertainty into a poem, sometimes but not necessarily with the suggestion that these conflicts can finally be resolved or reconciled

lyric originally a song accompanied by music (typically, the lyre); more generally, a poem expressing personal feelings (and often written in the first-person form), rather than telling a story

metaphor a figure of speech in which a word or phrase is applied to an object or action that it does not literally denote in order to imply a resemblance

metaphysical metaphysics is the philosophy of being and knowing, and in Donne's time concerned itself with such questions as the nature of the soul, and its relation to the body. Because Donne sometimes raised such questions in his love poems, some later critics, including John Dryden and Samuel Johnson, applied the term 'metaphysical' to the poems, with the suggestions that the poems were inappropriately ingenious and complicated (Dryden in particular seems to have thought that the women to whom love poems were supposedly addressed would merely be confused by intellectual arguments)

metre the rhythmic and regular arrangement of words and syllables

monosyllable a word of one syllable

New Criticism a literary critical style, and movement, which emphasised the skills of close reading, and sought to discuss 'the words on the page' rather than the author's intentions, the emotional affect of a work, or its historical or political context

Oedipus complex see Psychoanalytic criticism

persona the point of view or characteristics of the narrator

Petrarchan imitating the style and subject matter of the Italian poet Francesco Petrarca (1304–74), in particular his poems addressed to the idealised memory of a woman called Laura

post-structuralism a term covering the different approaches to language and literature initiated by Saussure. A basic tenet is that meaning is not inherent in words, but depends on their mutual relationships within the system of language, a system that is based on difference

proverb a short popular saying embodying a general truth, sometimes in metaphorical language

Psychoanalytic criticism Freud developed the theory of psychoanalysis as a means of curing neuroses in his patients, but its concepts were expanded by him and his followers as a means of understanding human behaviour and culture generally. Literature, for Freud, is produced by the same mechanism as dreams. Desires, mainly sexual, in conflict with social norms, are censored and pushed into the subconscious ('repression'), from which they emerge in forms (e.g. non-sexual goals like writing and painting) that are modified, disguised and all but unrecognisable to the conscious mind. The critic's task is to reveal the true latent content of literature, the psychological realities that underlie the work or art

pun usually defined as 'a play on words'; two widely different meanings are drawn out of a single word, usually for comic or playful purposes

quatrain a stanza of four lines, frequently though not always rhymed *abab*

rhyme chiming or matching sounds which create a very clearly audible sense of pattern

rhythm the chief element of rhythm is the variation in levels of stress accorded to the syllables

Romantic period a convenient term in English literary history for the period dating from 1789 to about 1830. See Romanticism

Romanticism/Romantic literary interests and attributes often used to contrast neo-classical literature, characterised by an emphasis of feeling and content rather than order and form, on the sublime supernatural and exotic, and the free expression of the passions and individuality

satire derived from the Latin satura, meaning a mixture, but now applied to poems or other writings in which vice or folly are held up to ridicule or censure; in Donne's lifetime, a false derivation (from the Greek 'satyr', a wood-god) was used to suggest that satirical verse should be rough or harsh in tone and diction

simile a figure of speech in which one thing is explicitly said to be like another; similes always contain the words 'like' or 'as'

sonnet a lyric poem in a fixed form, of fourteen lines (though some poets have modified this form), and often with a strictly defined rhyme scheme. Despite the title, none of John Donne's *Songs and Sonets* are in the sonnet form; in the *Holy Sonnets* John Donne uses a rhyme scheme modelled on Petrarch, with an octave (the first eight lines) rhymed *abbaabba*, and a sestet (the final six lines) rhymed *dedeff*

stanza a unit of several lines of verse; a repeated group of lines of verse

stress in any word of more than one syllable, more emphasis or loudness will be given to one of the syllables in comparison with the others. More significant words, such as nouns and verbs, tend to bear strong stress

syntax the arrangement of words in their appropriate forms and proper order, in order to achieve meaning

tone the mood, manner or attitude suggested by or embodied in a poem (e.g., serious, reflective, angry, bitter, etc.)

verse commonly refers to poetry in general, especially to denote metrical writing rather than prose

wit used in the seventeenth century for the capacity to link or combine ideas in new and original ways (as in the conceit), and sometimes opposed to judgement, or the capacity to separate and oppose ideas; from being almost the defining quality of poetic intelligence, wit came in the late eighteenth and nineteenth centuries to be associated with a kind of superficial cleverness which was considered the antithesis of poetical feeling or inspiration

AUTHOR OF THIS NOTE

Phillip Mallett read English at King's College, Cambridge, and is now Senior Lecturer in English at the University of St Andrews. He is the editor of Kipling's *Limits and Renewals*, and of various collections of essays, including *Kipling Considered, Satire*, and (with R.P. Draper) *A Spacious Vision: Essays on Thomas Hardy*. He is currently working on a study of John Ruskin.

GCSE and equivalent levels

Maya Angelou
I Know Why the Caged Bird Sings

Jane Austen
Pride and Prejudice

Alan Ayckbourn
Absent Friends

Elizabeth Barrett Browning
Selected Poems

Robert Bolt
A Man for All Seasons

Harold Brighouse
Hobson's Choice

Charlotte Brontë
Jane Eyre

Emily Brontë
Wuthering Heights

Shelagh Delaney
A Taste of Honey

Charles Dickens
David Copperfield

Charles Dickens
Great Expectations

Charles Dickens
Hard Times

Charles Dickens
Oliver Twist

Roddy Doyle
Paddy Clarke Ha Ha Ha

George Eliot
Silas Marner

George Eliot
The Mill on the Floss

William Golding
Lord of the Flies

Oliver Goldsmith
She Stoops To Conquer

Willis Hall
The Long and the Short and the Tall

Thomas Hardy
Far from the Madding Crowd

Thomas Hardy
The Mayor of Casterbridge

Thomas Hardy
Tess of the d'Urbervilles

Thomas Hardy
The Withered Arm and other Wessex Tales

L.P. Hartley
The Go-Between

Seamus Heaney
Selected Poems

Susan Hill
I'm the King of the Castle

Barry Hines
A Kestrel for a Knave

Louise Lawrence
Children of the Dust

Harper Lee
To Kill a Mockingbird

Laurie Lee
Cider with Rosie

Arthur Miller
The Crucible

Arthur Miller
A View from the Bridge

Robert O'Brien
Z for Zachariah

Frank O'Connor
My Oedipus Complex and other stories

George Orwell
Animal Farm

J.B. Priestley
An Inspector Calls

Willy Russell
Educating Rita

Willy Russell
Our Day Out

J.D. Salinger
The Catcher in the Rye

William Shakespeare
Henry IV Part 1

William Shakespeare
Henry V

William Shakespeare
Julius Caesar

William Shakespeare
Macbeth

William Shakespeare
The Merchant of Venice

William Shakespeare
A Midsummer Night's Dream

William Shakespeare
Much Ado About Nothing

William Shakespeare
Romeo and Juliet

William Shakespeare
The Tempest

William Shakespeare
Twelfth Night

George Bernard Shaw
Pygmalion

Mary Shelley
Frankenstein

R.C. Sherriff
Journey's End

Rukshana Smith
Salt on the snow

John Steinbeck
Of Mice and Men

Robert Louis Stevenson
Dr Jekyll and Mr Hyde

Jonathan Swift
Gulliver's Travels

Robert Swindells
Daz 4 Zoe

Mildred D. Taylor
Roll of Thunder, Hear My Cry

Mark Twain
Huckleberry Finn

James Watson
Talking in Whispers

William Wordsworth
Selected Poems

A Choice of Poets

Mystery Stories of the Nineteenth Century including The Signalman

Nineteenth Century Short Stories

Poetry of the First World War

Six Women Poets

York Notes Advanced

Margaret Atwood
The Handmaid's Tale

Jane Austen
Mansfield Park

Jane Austen
Persuasion

Jane Austen
Pride and Prejudice

Alan Bennett
Talking Heads

William Blake
Songs of Innocence and of Experience

Charlotte Brontë
Jane Eyre

Emily Brontë
Wuthering Heights

Geoffrey Chaucer
The Franklin's Tale

Geoffrey Chaucer
General Prologue to the Canterbury Tales

Geoffrey Chaucer
The Wife of Bath's Prologue and Tale

Joseph Conrad
Heart of Darkness

Charles Dickens
Great Expectations

John Donne
Selected Poems

George Eliot
The Mill on the Floss

F. Scott Fitzgerald
The Great Gatsby

E.M. Forster
A Passage to India

Brian Friel
Translations

Thomas Hardy
The Mayor of Casterbridge

Thomas Hardy
Tess of the d'Urbervilles

Seamus Heaney
Selected Poems from Opened Ground

Nathaniel Hawthorne
The Scarlet Letter

James Joyce
Dubliners

John Keats
Selected Poems

Christopher Marlowe
Doctor Faustus

Arthur Miller
Death of a Salesman

Toni Morrison
Beloved

William Shakespeare
Antony and Cleopatra

William Shakespeare
As You Like It

William Shakespeare
Hamlet

William Shakespeare
King Lear

William Shakespeare
Measure for Measure

William Shakespeare
The Merchant of Venice

William Shakespeare
Much Ado About Nothing

William Shakespeare
Othello

William Shakespeare
Romeo and Juliet

William Shakespeare
The Tempest

William Shakespeare
The Winter's Tale

Mary Shelley
Frankenstein

Alice Walker
The Color Purple

Oscar Wilde
The Importance of Being Earnest

Tennessee Williams
A Streetcar Named Desire

John Webster
The Duchess of Malfi

W.B. Yeats
Selected Poems